D153

VISUALIZA⋯
AND GUIDED IMAGERY
FOR PAIN MANAGEMENT

R.D. LONGACRE, Ph.D., F.B.H.A

National Board for Hypnotherapy
and Hyponotic Anaesthesiology

KENDALL/HUNT PUBLISHING COMPANY
4050 Westmark Drive Dubuque, Iowa 52004

To my best friend, helpmate and wife, Sheila, who helped me push the clouds away and to my daughter, Leslie Nicole who makes the sun shine on a rainy day.

Thank you Dr. Miriam Spear for your guidance and support.

Contents

Foreword

―――――――――――――――――■―――――――――――――――――

From the time of its earliest use by prehistoric man, hypnosis has been endowed by both friend and foe with magical powers and supernatural proclivities. As a consequence of these attitudes, hypnosis is susceptible to unwarranted condemnation and outright distortion on the one hand and to uncontrolled wishful thinking on the other.

Too often, books on hypnosis written for the general public are a poorly compiled compendium of half-truths based more on tradition than on knowledge. This information packed volume is a welcome and refreshing change.

The author of this book is a professional hypnotherapist who takes much of the mystery out of hypnosis as he describes its applications in childbirth, anaesthesia, hypnodontics and pain management. Dr. Longacre shares with the reader the wealth of knowledge he has gained in his many years of experience as he describes several interesting and relevant case studies of his patients.

The reader will be pleased to find the information presented in a well-written, easy-to-understand format that describes in a "hands-on, how to" manner exactly how it is done. Dr. Longacre has accomplished his purpose to present to the lay and professional public both a comprehensive overview and a set of detailed instructions in the use of hypnosis in the clinical setting as it applies to childbirth, anaesthesia, hypnodontics and pain control. He does this simply and clearly, using examples from his own clinical experience. He has selected his material well. His explanation of the material is excellent.

This book is worthy of attention and study by anyone interested in hypnosis. Those al ready involved in hypnosis will appreciate this serious contribution to the field.

Caroline Miller, Ph.D.
Past Vice President, National Board for Hypnotherary and Hypnotic Anaesthesiology

Preface

I first became interested in the clinical application of hypnosis for childbirth, anaesthesia and pain management while working in the various intensive care units of the University of California Irvine Medical Center in Orange, California.

As a Respiratory Care Practitioner, I was often called upon to perform procedures that were painful or unpleasant for the patient. In many cases pain medication mediated patient discomfort but all too often these patients still experienced varying degrees of tension and anxiety that could not be alleviated with medication. I mentioned my concern about these patients to an anaesthesiology resident who recommended that I investigate the work of William A. Kroger M.D., who had published several volumes on clinical hypnosis.

Dr. Kroger's work in the area of clinical hypnosis inspired me to take a basic course in hypnotherapy and then pursue a graduate degree in this holistic health modality.

I was amazed at the dramatic results of hypnotherapy in the hospital setting for alleviation of patient tension, fear and anxiety. Adults and children responded to guided imagery for amelioration of pain.

When my wife announced that she was carrying our first child and was fearful of the pain of childbirth, I exhausted the literature on hypnotic natural childbirth and interviewed countless childbirth professionals. The results of my research and experience is presented in this book.

The knowledge you can gain by carefully studying this material will be invaluable in helping childbirth patients as well as those seen for dentistry or chronic pain alleviation.

Students who have attended my continuing education courses, seminars or training sessions report success in helping others help themselves with clinical hypnosis.

Clinical hypnotherapists and registered nurses who have attended my classes, approved by the California Board of Registered Nursing, also report excellent results and support the efficacy of hypnotherapy in health care.

Many medical doctors, psychiatrists, dentists and psychologists are now employing hypnotherapists in their private practices. These health professionals require well trained hypnotherapists.

I trust you will find this book to be a valuable tool in your practice of hypnotic childbirth, dentistry or pain management.

R.D. Longacre, Ph.D., F.B.H.A.

Introduction

What does the term "Visualization and Guided Imagery" mean? There may be more than a hundred different definitions to describe visualization and guided imagery used by physicians, psychologists, allied health professionals and practitioners of various holistic or "new age" health modalities. Perhaps the best explanation will be determined by you when you investigate what "Visualization and Guided Imagery" is not.

Visualization and guided imagery is not a mind power or mind control technique or a method to circumvent traditional medical and psychological medicine.

Visualization and guided imagery is not a new advertising slogan or the foundation for a new spiritual movement.

Visualization and guided imagery is not a complicated set of rules and instructions that require hours of practice, concentration and expensive study materials.

VISUALIZATION AND GUIDED IMAGERY IS A

NATURAL AND NORMAL PROCESS THAT YOU USE

EVERYDAY WHEN MAKING DECISIONS FOR YOURSELF

The concepts of "Visualization and Guided Imagery" presented in this book are as old as scriptures in the Bible, as meaningful as the proven wisdom of pioneers of modern American technology and as new as the modern techniques of Complementary Medicine.

The concepts of Visualization and Guided Imagery are based on a belief system that you develop to fit your own personal life plan for living. In other words, using visualization and guided imagery is as simple as picturing and imagining something you desire and then allowing yourself to enjoy this picture or image as if it was already completed.

Religious people may identify with the phrase, "Whatsoever you ask, believing that you shall receive."

Entrepreneurs and those working in business may discover the meaning of visualization and guided imagery by reflecting on the quote attributed to Henry Ford, "Think you can, think you can't, either way you're right."

Painful medical and emotional problems can be ameliorated or alleviated with positive thinking or believing in your ability to use visualization and guided imagery to create changes you desire in your mind or body.

THIS IS A BOOK ABOUT MAKING NEW THINGS HAPPEN IN YOUR LIFE

This book is the result of over ten years of research and interaction with professionals in a variety of health care disciplines. The basic chapters of the book were written as a clinical training manual for physicians and nurses working with patients suffering from unnecessary or unwanted pain or chronic pain conditions that required more than prescriptions for pain medication.

The original training manual was titled, "The Principles and Clinical Applications of Hypnosis for Childbirth, Anaesthesia and Pain Management." Thousands of health care professionals have used the concepts of the original title in their private practice of medicine, psychology, nursing, pastoral care and hypnotherapy.

The basic cognitive process of visualization and guided imagery is much the same as the ethical medical and psychological applications of hypnosis. For this reason the terms "hypnosis," "hypnotherapy" and "imagery" are used in this book so as not to detract from the original manuscript.

Visualization and guided imagery is a client- or patient-centered approach to total wellness. This approach is also referred to as client- or patient-directed. The techniques and concepts in this book do not require that an individual be hypnotized or pay for the services of a medical doctor, psychiatrist or licensed mental health counselors.

Visualization and guided imagery is a self-help teaching modality that can be used as an adjunct to traditional medicine or psychotherapy.

Information about Visualization and Guided Imagery as a Self-Help, Holistic and Complementary Medical Modality is available from the National Board for Hypnotherapy and Hypnotic Anaesthesiology.

CHAPTER 1

Hypnosis for Childbirth, Anaesthesia and Pain Management

———————————————■———————————————

"Just relax." Almost every health care practitioner has given this advice at one time or another to a patient or client. The goal of the hypnotherapist or allied health professional using the principles and clinical application of hypnosis and guided imagery is to teach clients and patients how to use their own God-given abilities and subconscious mind to facilitate deep relaxation and employ guided imagery techniques that may enable them to overcome problems that are affecting their lives.

Therapeutic hypnosis is an accepted and viable modality in the care and treatment of numerous health problems and related diseases. Hypnotherapy is used by medical doctors, psychiatrists, dentists and psychologists. Hypnotherapy is a valuable tool for nursing and allied health professionals to promote wellness.

Therapeutic hypnosis has been proven to be effective in the treatment or alleviation of problems associated with psychosomatic cardiovascular disorders and coronary disease.

The efficacy of hypnotherapy has also been demonstrated in the treatment of gastrointestinal disorders, arthritis, metabolic diseases, obesity, hyperthyroidism, anorexia nervosa, alcoholism, respiratory disorders, bronchial asthma and a variety of allergies that may or may not have a psychogenic component.

Hypnosis can provide analgesia for general surgery, dental surgery and a variety of invasive diagnostic procedures. Hypnotherapy can also benefit oncology, orthopedic, rehabilitation, intensive care and pediatric patients.

Therapeutic hypnosis is a viable modality for psychiatrists and psychologists in the treatment of mental health disorders. Hypnotherapy is also beneficial for behavior modification therapy in the treatment of substance abuse.

Therapeutic hypnosis is applicable in many areas of nursing care. Surgical patients can gain confidence that the procedure being performed will have positive results, thereby reducing preoperative fear and anxiety. Post-operative problems such as urine retention, nausea and pain can be ameliorated. Post-operative discomfort due to sitting, standing or ambulating can be alleviated.

Hypnotherapy can help intensive care patients gain much needed periods of rest and relaxation. Patients in CCU with cardio-vascular insults such as supraventricular arrhythmias, paroxysmal tachycardia and ventricular ectopic beats can benefit from hypnotic relaxation and guided imagery.

Hypnosis is useful in psychiatric nursing to teach agitated and depressed patients how to relax and alleviate hurtful stress and tension.

Hypnotic relaxation and imagery can be applied in rehabilitation nursing to teach patients preventative and restorative skills.

Hypnotherapy is applicable in trauma care to facilitate diagnostic procedures in the E.R. and for the treatment of hypercapnia.

In the doctor's office, hypnotherapy can minimize pain associated with injections or diagnostic procedures, potentiate medications and traditional therapy for certain dermatological conditions.

An Overview of the History of Hypnosis

If hypnosis is such a valuable tool for the health professions, why was it neglected for centuries? One explanation is that in the evolution of all scientific learning there has been one constant factor; superstition precedes knowledge.

Magic alchemy preceded modern chemistry. Alchemy was the philosophical and magical association to chemistry in the middle ages. The alchemists attempted to turn base metals into gold and discover the elixir of youth. The occult science of astrology was the forerunner of modern astronomy. It took a long period of time for the belief in the curative powers of witch doctors to be transferred to modern day physicians.

Generally a new idea must pass through three phases before it is accepted. At first the idea is thought to be impossible. Then the idea is considered sacrilegious or preposterous. Finally the idea is axiomatic; everyone knew it would work long before the idea was generally accepted.

Hypnosis stalled in phase two due to the antics of the early experimenters.

Evolution Of Hypnosis

A Greek engraving dated 928 BC shows Chiron, the most renowned physician of his time, placing his pupil, Aesculapius, in a hypnotic trance.

The Delphic Oracle and other ancient writings by priests and men of wisdom postulated the curative power of hypnosis whether self-induced or induced with drugs or volcanic fumes.

In 1773, Frederick Anton Mesmer presented to the Faculty of Medicine of the University of Vienna, his thesis on "The Influence Of The Stars And Planets As Curative Powers." Mesmer claimed that the moon, sun and stars affected the human organism through an invisible fluid which he called animal magnetism.

Mesmer claimed that the benefits of animal magnetism included miraculous health cures. Popular belief in his claims became so wide spread that he was forced to invent a primitive form of mass production.

Mesmer used large *baquets*, a French word for tubs, filled with water to induce hypnosis. Allegedly, the water in the tubs had magnetic properties. Metal rods protruded from these tubs and when the patient touched a rod, they experienced hysterical outbursts and found relief from their malady or were cured. Several of these tubs were placed in a room and a large group of patients could be "Mesmerized" while spectators watched with amusement from a balcony above the treatment room.

Mesmer did not understand why, but the principles of hypnosis helped his patients. Unfortunately Mesmer was soon out of business and discredited by the scientific community due to the carnival nature of his practice.

Mesmer's name lives on in England where the term Mesmerized is preferred over the term hypnotized. The word hypnosis was derived from the Greek word *hypnos* which means sleep.

Many of the early pioneers of hypnosis used methods that were almost as remarkable as Mesmer's techniques. The principles of hypnosis were operative in a variety of curative concepts with resultant acceptance or rejection until the scientific community accepted hypnotherapy as a viable modality in the care and management of patients or clients in the 1950s.

Early Pioneers In Europe

The Marquis De Puysegur, a former student of Mesmer, revived some of the ideas about hypnosis that had shrunk into oblivion. He demonstrated artificial somnambulism instead of hysterical outbursts associated with Mesmer.

Father Gassner, a Jesuit priest who lived in Southern Germany, used unusual methods to induce hypnosis and reported spectacular cures.

Dr. James Braid, a prominent Manchester, England surgeon, is considered to be the father of the scientific evolution of hypnosis for writing "Doctrine of Suggestion."

Dr. Burcq, a French physician, used polished brass knobs to induce hypnosis. A French neurologist, Dr. Luys, investigated Burcq's work and later developed the revolving mirror for the production of somnambulistic sleep.

Dr. Charcot, another French neurologist who investigated Burcq's theories, made the first attempt to scientifically classify hypnotic phenomena by successfully proving that there are several stages of hypnotic sleep and that the hypnotized subject is capable of manifesting various symptoms or clinical signs at each stage.

Sigmund Freud studied and used hypnosis early in his career but then abandoned the modality because he could not incorporate the phenomena into his own hypnotherapeutic method of psycho-analysis.

Ambroisé Auguste Liebeault and Hippolyt Marie Bernheim are considered to be the legitimate inventors of modern psychotherapy as well as hypnotherapy. They considered hypnosis to be a function of normal behavior and introduced the concept of suggestion and suggestibility.

Dr. Racamier, a French surgeon, reported in 1821 the successful application of hypnosis for anaesthesia. The doctor operated on patients after placing them in a Mesmeric Coma.

Early Pioneers In America

The early relationship between the introduction of hypnosis and chemical anaesthesia in the United States is interesting. Both were introduced by stage performers or so called itinerant chemists or street corner professors in the mid 1800s.

Gardner Q. Colton, an itinerant chemist, gave an exhibition in Hartford, Connecticut on December 11, 1844. Mr. Colton used laughing gas to place subjects appearing in his stage show in a hypnotic state. During the show a young man under the influence of laughing gas stumbled against a chair and badly bruised his legs. Mr. Colton terminated the hypnotic trance and sent the young man back to his seat in the audience.

Ironically the young man's seat was next to a seat occupied by a dentist. The dentist, Dr. Wells, observed that though the young man's legs were badly bruised and bloody, he reported no sensation of pain until the effects of the laughing gas wore off.

The following day Dr. Wells asked one of his colleagues, Dr. Riggs, to assist him in an experiment. Dr. Wells allowed himself to be anesthetized with laughing gas (nitrous oxide) and then instructed Dr. Riggs to extract a tooth while he was under the influence of the gas. Like the young man at the exhibition, the doctor did not experience any pain until the effects of the laughing gas wore off.

One hundred years later, dentists were using hypnosis for anaesthesia and as an adjunct modality for patient relaxation and dental care.

Various metaphysical and religious healing movements in Europe spread to America in the early 1900s. The principles of hypnosis were a part of many of these curative concepts.

Phineas Quimby, who is associated with the evolution of the Christian Science Church, practiced healing methods developed in Europe by the Chevalier de Barbarin, who magnetized people. Quimby attracted many disciples. One of Quimby's supporters was Mary Baker Eddy who is one of the principle founders of the Christian Science Church.

It is interesting to note that modern day Christian Scientists are opposed to the use of hypnosis for medical or healing purposes. The principles of hypnosis are employed by Christian Science Practitioners but they deny that their method of treatment was or is associated with hypnotic principles or techniques.

Hypnosis and Modern Medicine

The need for rapid treatment of battle neurosis during World War II and the Korean Conflict created a renewed interest in the clinical application of hypnosis. Various medical and psychological disciplines began investigating the efficacy of hypnotherapy for their respective patients. Dentists were also prominent proponents of therapeutic hypnosis.

Aaron A. Moss D.D.S., and a group of colleagues banded together to spread the gospel of hypnosis in dentistry. In order to dispel the superstitions and myths about clinical hypnosis, Dr. Moss coined the term hypnodontics.

In 1955, the British Medical Association approved the use of hypnosis for the treatment of psychoneurosis and for anaesthesia during surgery for childbirth.

On September 13, 1958, the Council on Mental Health of the American Medical Association recommended; in view of our increasing knowledge, hypnosis instruction be included in the curricula of medical schools and post graduate training centers. In 1961 the AMA gave further approval for the use of clinical hypnotherapy by recommending a minimum of 144 hours of training in hypnotherapy for student physicians and medical doctors.

Today hypnosis is considered a valuable tool for health care professionals. Hypnosis is an important aspect of holistic health care. The efficacy of hypnotherapy has been documented by respected health care organizations and regulatory agencies.

CHAPTER 2

The Psychophysiological Aspects of Hypnosis

There are many theories and conceptual models regarding the psychophysiological aspects of hypnosis. When reviewing the literature, one could easily assume that there are as many theories as their are investigators of hypnotic phenomena. The purpose of this chapter is not to hypothesize a new theory or offer evidence to support an existing one. The following conceptual model of the psychophysiological aspects of hypnosis is presented to aid the practitioner of hypnotic childbirth, anaesthesia and pain management in explaining to patients how and why hypnosis works.

Hemispheres of the Brain

A basic conceptual model of hypnotic psychophysiology assumes that reality and perceptual awareness is perceived from inside the brain rather than from the outside or physical environment. This model, "Right Brain/Left Brain," portrays the mind as having two divisions; the left hemisphere and the right hemisphere.

The left hemisphere of the brain is the conscious or cortical portion of the mind. The left hemisphere deals with the analysis of input, logic and reasoning. The right hemisphere deals with abstract thoughts; art, music, imagery and fundamental learning.

The two hemispheres of the brain are interrelated physiologically. The left brain or cortical portion reacts with the right brain or subcortical portion.

Cortical input is sent to the subcortical part of the brain for validation of reality or stored memory data. Subcortical centers then send information about memory or data to the cortical centers, which then instigate physiological actions or reactions.

The autonomic nervous system reportedly is part of the subcortical areas of the brain and does not require conscious or left brain control in order to perform its assigned functions. Several demonstrations of voluntary control of the autonomic (also termed involuntary) nervous system have substantiated the interrelationship of the conscious and subconscious mind

External input to the brain is facilitated by neurons and transduced chemically to the conscious mind for analysis. If the conscious mind determines that no immediate action is necessary, the information is stored in the data banks of the subconscious.

All of the physiological responses of the body are triggered by the brain which causes the release of a variety of chemicals that produce physiological responses. In other words, what the brain perceives as reality and acts upon, the body must do.

The left brain/right brain concept assumes that only the mind can think and once a physiological response is initiated, the body must obey its master, the mind, like a robot. If input to the brain bypasses the cortical or analytical process and reaches the subconscious while the patient or client is in a state of hypnosis, desired physiological responses must occur.

An example of the body is a robot phenomena is the lemon suggestibility test. If you concentrate on the palm of your hand and imagine that you are holding a freshly picked, bright yellow lemon, you should be able to demonstrate your mind's ability to trigger a physiological response.

Allow yourself to concentrate on the palm of one of your hands and picture and imagine a lovely, fresh, bright, aromatic lemon. Visualize and feel the lemon in the palm of your hand. Feel the moist juice of the lemon as you imagine that you are cutting it in half. Picture and imagine now that the lemon is cut in half and visualize the pulp of the lemon and feel the texture of the peel. Now put your hand to your mouth and take a big bite out of the lemon. If your subconscious mind accepted the idea that you were holding and then biting into the lemon, your mouth probably salivated as it would if the lemon had been real rather than imagined.

Therapeutic hypnosis allows the conscious mind to rest and narrow the focus of concentration rather than analyze input to determine whether it is real or imagined. When the mind is in a hypnotic state, suggestions given by the therapist that are in the patient's or client's best interest, are accepted. When a suggestion is accepted a physiological response occurs.

Stages of Hypnosis

The depth of hypnosis that a patient or client can achieve may be classified according to the physiological responses observed by the health care practitioner or hypnotherapist. There are four basic stages or depths of hypnosis; hypnoidal (pre-hypnotic), light stage, medium stage and deep stage.

Hypnoidal Stage

During the hypnoidal stage the subject is aware of everything going on around them and finds distracting influences disturbing. The subject will obey simple suggestions but will not react favorably to complicated suggestions. As this stage deepens, the subject becomes extremely relaxed and appears drowsy, although they may not feel affected.

Physiological responses include; closing of the eyes, fluttering of the eyelids, heaviness of limbs and complete physical relaxation.

Light stage

The light stage is sufficient for many therapeutic goals. The subject makes little effort to resist suggestions and simple post hypnotic suggestions are heeded.

Physiological responses include; catalepsy of the eyes, partial limb catalepsy, inhibition of small muscle groups, slower and deeper breathing, slower pulse rate, twitching of the mouth or jaw and twitching of the extremities during induction.

Medium stage

The medium stage suffices for almost any therapeutic goal. Subjects should not be taken to a deeper stage unless the operator is well-trained and has the necessary clinical experience.

Physiological responses in this stage include; complete muscular inhibition and kinesthetic delusions, partial amnesia, glove anaesthesia, tactile, gustatory and olfactory illusions, hyperacuity to atmospheric conditions and complete catalepsy of limbs or the body.

Deep stage

The deep stage of hypnosis is seldom indicated for clinical hypnotherapy. Specialists in hypnotic anaesthesia take patients to a deep stage of hypnosis to facilitate analgesia for surgery. This deep state is not dangerous for the patient but it can present potential problems and a frustrating experience for the therapist.

Subjects in a deep state of hypnosis often take an "I don't give a damn" attitude about the therapist's suggestions.

Physiological responses include; the ability to open the eyes without affecting the trance, pupillary dilation and fixed stare when the eyes are open, somnambulism, complete amnesia and complete anaesthesia. In this deep state, bizarre post hypnotic suggestions are carried out and organic body functions such as heart rate, blood pressure and metabolic functions can be subconsciously controlled or regulated. The recall of lost memories, hypermnesia, can also be observed

Pain Control Theories

There are three conceptual theories that offer a basic explanation of the psychophysiology of hypnosis for anaesthesia and pain management. These theories also provide an explanation of the psychoneurological aspects of hypnotic anaesthesia.

Control Gate Theory

The control gate theory postulates that pain impulses traveling to the mind must pass through a control gate or valve before reaching a command center in the left brain. This command center or switchboard analyzes the information and then channels the pain stimuli to appropriate pain response centers that instigate a physiological response.

When the left brain or conscious side of the mind has a narrowed focus or span of attention, the control gate allows only wanted or selected pain impulses to enter and trigger a physiological response, i.e., the sensation of pain.

The control gate closes when the attention of the conscious mind is misdirected or centered on a fixed focus such as the therapist's voice or a visual object, real or imagined.

The control gate theory assumes that physiological pain is ignored by the mind due to an increase of the individual's pain threshold

ANS Inhibition Theory

The autonomic (involuntary) nervous system has two branches or sides; the sympathetic and the parasympathetic. The sympathetic side is the fight or flight branch. The parasympathetic side is the relaxation branch

Emotional or physical stimulation of the sympathetic side results in accelerated breathing and heart rate as well as psychological survival instincts and behaviors. The sympathetic side of the ANS responds to tension, anxiety, fear and pain. The parasympathetic side of the ANS triggers the relaxation response. With relaxation the breathing and heart rate returns to a normal range and minor discomfort is ignored as the body recuperates from a stressful experience.

The ANS Inhibition Theory suggests that with hypnosis, the sympathetic branch can be controlled by the parasympathetic or relaxation side. In other words, the relaxation response can inhibit or ameliorate pain stimuli. With deep relaxation pain can be interpreted as pressure by the mind.

The Body Is A Robot Theory

This theory is easily understood by patients or clients and presents a good explanation of hypnotic pain control phenomena.

"The Body is a Robot Theory" assumes that only the mind can think and the body is a robot controlled by the mind. Therefore, what the mind chooses to accept or perceive as reality, the body must do.

If the subconscious mind accepts that pain is only pressure then the body's physiological response must be a response to pressure rather than pain.

An example of this theory is a person walking barefoot on a beautiful white sandy beach. Their conscious attention is focused on the smell of the sea breeze and the waves. They feel the sand beneath their feet and the sun warming their face as they walk along enjoying their stroll. Inadvertently they step on a small sharp shell or pebble but do not feel pain, only pressure.

In this example the mind has narrowed its focus and is accepting auto-suggestions that the walk on the beach is a pleasurable experience. Therefore the sharp shell or pebble is interpreted by the subconscious mind as minor discomfort that did not warrant a sympathetic or pain stimuli response.

The foot stepping on the sharp object did not perceive the object as a source of pain because only the mind can think or react to pain stimuli.

CHAPTER 3

General Indications, Precautions and Contraindications

———————————————■———————————————

Many different types of patients can benefit from hypnotherapy while in the hospital. Hypnotherapy is indicated for almost all areas of nursing care.

The use of hypnosis in preoperative patient management can help the surgical patient overcome anxiety and alleviate the fear of surgery. Hypnotherapy can instill patient confidence that the surgery being done will progress without complications and have a positive outcome. Post operatively, the patient can be guided into comfortable sitting, standing and ambulation without unnecessary pain. Hypnotherapy may also be used to alleviate problems associated with poor appetite.

Hypnotherapy is beneficial for intensive care patients. Relaxation and guided imagery can help these patients gain periods of much needed rest, thereby preventing ICU narcoses. Hypnosis is useful to alleviate pain related to injections or the drawing of blood samples, including arterial blood gas punctures. Hypnotherapy can also be used to potentiate medications and enhance the patient's general comfort and sense of well-being.

Hypnotherapy has many clinical applications in rehabilitation nursing. The rehabilitation patient who is relaxed, comfortable and has a positive self image tends to participate more fully in rehabilitation therapy.

In general nursing, hypnotherapy can help increase patient mobility, simple range of motion exercises and activities of daily living. Patients recovering from an amputation or orthopedic injury can use hypnosis to improve mobility, limb control and walking. General surgery patients can regain bowel and bladder control in a shorter period of time by using hypnosis.

Hypnotherapy is indicated for patients presenting in the emergency room or trauma center. Diagnostic procedures can be more readily accomplished if the patient is relaxed and is not experiencing unnecessary anxiety, tension or fear. With hypnotic relaxation, the insertion of catheters or injections are more easily tolerated. Hypnosis can also help acute asthma patients overcome the fear and panic related to shortness of breath and in some cases even facilitate the relaxation and subsequent dilation of bronchial smooth muscle.

Hypnosis is highly indicated to help confused patients focus their attention and provide clear and concise answers to questions regarding their medical history and the nature of their presenting complaint.

In the medical office, hypnotherapy is indicated for the alleviation of tension, anxiety and pain. White coat hypertension, abnormally high blood pressure due to anxiety, can be alleviated with hypnosis. Hypnotic relaxation imagery often can reverse the decompensating spiral of tension and muscle spasm associated with asthma and chronic lung diseases.

Post hypnotic suggestions can enhance the effects of oral medications or injections prescribed by the physician.

Hypnotic glove anaesthesia can provide relief from itching for dermatological conditions such as neurodermatitis. Psoriasis can be helped with guided imagery that duplicates the sensation of sun and heat.

Precautions

Health practitioners who use hypnotherapy and guided imagery to help or treat patients or clients must always remember that hypnosis is not a form of sleep or a dulled state of awareness. The patient in a hypnotic state is actually in a state of heightened awareness and suggestibility. Therefore, words such as pain, hurt and other negative expressions must be avoided.

If a post hypnotic suggestion is given only to determine the depth of hypnosis achieved by the patient, this suggestion must be removed before the therapy session is terminated.

When formulating hypnotic and post hypnotic suggestions, the therapist must choose their words carefully. The hypnotized patient or client reacts to words literally.

Contraindications

There are few contraindications for hypnotherapy. It is generally accepted that hypnosis is a self-induced state and the therapist only guides the patient or client to enable them to reach this state of deep relaxation and increased concentration. Therefore, the patient or client is always in complete control and will accept suggestions given by the therapist only if these suggestions are in the patient's or client's best interest

In a state of hypnosis, the patient's own physiological defense mechanisms and social values or mores will prevent the occurrence of any potentially harmful act occasioned by the therapist's suggestions.

Specific contraindications for hypnotherapy are predicated on the therapist's training, skill, experience and the clinical objective of therapy.

When working in the areas of hypnotic anaesthesia, hypnodontics and pain management, direct symptom removal of pain is always contraindicated without the approval of a physician.

Direct symptom removal of pain may not cause immediate injury or harm to the patient, however, it may delay the patient from seeking proper medical advice.

Hypnotic anaesthesia therapy should only be undertaken by a therapist who has been well-trained in this specialty area and has demonstrated professional competence and clinical ability.

CHAPTER 4

The Clinical Interview

The purpose of the clinical interview is to determine the therapeutic objective, appropriate therapeutic suggestions and the preferred method for the induction of hypnosis.

The therapeutic objective must include the patient's expectations, belief and desired results of hypnotherapy. Hypnotherapy can not create, instigate or facilitate results that the patient does not really want. If the patient expects the therapist to make them want a given result, the positive aspects of therapy are nullified. In other words, the prognosis for therapeutic results follows the principles of the law of self-fulfilling prophecy. This law states that whatever the patient desires and expects to happen will probably happen.

If a patient or client expects that you can make them desire something that they really do not want, the law of self fulfilling prophecy will prevent them from benefiting from therapy.

When a patient makes a statement such as; "Can you make me," "My wife wants me to," "My husband wants me to," "People have told me," they are probably stating a desire for negative therapeutic results.

Patients who express a desire for negative results should be referred to a psychologist or psychotherapist for evaluation and counseling before formulating a hypnotherapy treatment plan.

Hypnotic and post hypnotic suggestions must be formulated to fit the patient's vocabulary and language skills as well as their life experiences. During the clinical interview you should determine the patient's language ability and formulate suggestions that are within the boundary of their comprehension.

The patient's life experiences will enable you to determine the best method of hypnotic induction. If the patient is employed as an office clerk or in a situation where they customarily take orders, i.e., soldier, policeman or ancillary personnel, an authoritative approach is indicated. A permissive approach to hypnotic induction is indicated for patients accustomed to giving orders. Examples of this type of patient are lawyers, doctors, administrators and business executives.

Learning Systems

When formulating therapeutic suggestions, consideration should also be given to a patient's preferred mode of learning. The three basic modes of learning are visual, auditory and kinesthetic.

Visual refers to the sense of sight. Auditory refers to the sense of hearing and kinesthetic to the sense of feeling both emotionally and physically. These primary learning systems are organized in each individual in the following manner.

One of the systems will be the person's primary or highly developed system. Another system will serve them as a secondary or strong back-up system. The third system may or may not be used to access information

To determine an individual patient's primary learning or information accessing system, ask them an abstract question that requires more than a yes or no answer. Observe their eye movement and speech patterns when they respond to your question.

Visual

When visual people are asked a question that requires more than a yes or no answer, they will blink and then move their eyes up and to the left, up and to the right or look straight ahead before giving an answer.

Visual people speak in terms of seeing or watching. Some examples are; "I see what you mean," "I can't see that" and "It looks good." They will give vivid descriptions of things as though they are painting a word picture.

Visual people tend to require eye to eye contact when having a conversation and have a tendency to point to something or show you something as they speak.

Auditory

When auditory people respond to an abstract question they will generally blink and then look down and to the left or across the horizon before they answer.

Auditory people tend to speak in terms of sounds and hearing. Some examples are; "Listen to what I have to say," "That sounds good," "I hear what you mean" and "Did you hear about."

Auditory people seem to enjoy making noise. They often jingle coins or keys in their pockets, scuffle their feet and walk loudly. They like to repeat questions or statements before answering. For example, if you ask an auditory person, "What time is it?" they will repeat the question and then answer it. They will often laugh at the punch line of a joke and then repeat it. Their voices may also trail off when they are speaking.

An auditory person does not seem to need the eye to eye contact that a visual person does. When talking with an auditory person you may think that they are ignoring you but that is generally not the case. Auditory people are usually so busy explaining their point or idea that they don't have time to listen to you.

When you want an auditory person to really listen to what you are saying, it is best to make sure you have their attention before you begin speaking.

Kinesthetic

Kinesthetic people will usually look down and to the right before answering a complex question.

They often speak in terms of feelings both emotional and physical. You may hear statements like, "I can't get a handle on my life," "I can't grasp that" or "I feel like."

Kinesthetic people, like auditory people, do not seem to need eye to eye contact during a conversation. However, they do seem to have a tendency to touch a lot, both themselves and others. They also seem to have a need to be touched by others.

Accessing System Hierarchy

People often go through all of their learning or accessing systems when searching for an answer to a question. Generally they will use their primary accessing system first and then their secondary or back-up system. Auditory people tend to develop a back-up system almost as strong as their primary system which can be confusing even for the most observant therapist.

In general, men tend to be visual and or auditory while women are generally kinesthetic.

By recognizing a person's primary learning system, you can establish a greater degree of rapport in the therapeutic setting and formulate more effective imagery for hypnotherapy.

The best method or technique for the induction of hypnosis may also be determined during the clinical interview. The preferred method of induction employed should always enhance the patient's expectations, belief and desired results from therapy. The three basic methods of hypnotic induction that are generally used for hypnotic anaesthesia, hypnodontics, childbirth and pain management can be classified as direct, indirect and disguised.

A direct induction method is used when a patient has had a previous experience with hypnosis and has established a degree of rapport with the therapist. Direct induction is usually facilitated with a post hypnotic suggestion during the initial therapy session. This post hypnotic suggestion might be, "When I see you again you will be able to deeply relax, even deeper relaxed than you are now, when I touch your right shoulder and say sleep."

An indirect method of induction is indicated for patients who have not had a previous experience with hypnosis or have had a disagreeable experience with a previous therapist. Indirect induction requires the therapist to give a comprehensive explanation of how hypnosis works, why it works and what the patient can expect from therapy. It is important to dispel the myriad of myths about hypnosis that the patient may have come to believe.

A disguised method of induction is indicated when the patient's problem predicates urgency, i.e., emergency situation, or if their age or physical condition, understanding of hypnosis or potential objections inhibits them from fully cooperating with the therapist.

A disguised method of induction is contraindicated unless the hypnotherapist is working under the direction of a physician and has the necessary training and experience in hypnotic anaesthesia to employ this method utilizing a variety of disguised induction techniques.

Clinical Interview Protocol

The clinical interview is usually conducted as part of the preinduction visit. The term clinical interview refers to that portion of the initial therapy session that is used to get to know the patient, establish rapport and determine therapeutic goals.

The following protocol has proven to be effective for establishing therapeutic goals and maximizing the benefits of therapy.

1. Solicit information about the patient's occupation, hobbies and special interests.

2. Inquire about the patient's previous experience with hypnosis or their familiarity with the phenomena.

3. Determine if the patient really wants the expected outcome of therapy.

4. Establish rapport with the patient by telling them a little about your training and past experience in helping people with a similar problem.

5. Explain to the patient how you plan to help them with their problem and the results they can expect from therapy.

6. Ask the patient if they want you to help them overcome their problem.

7. Listen to the patient's choice of words and tone of voice during the interview. Watch for expressions both verbal and nonverbal that may provide clues as to their primary learning system. Remember that all hypnosis is really self-hypnosis and the patient will usually only achieve the results they honestly want and desire.

CHAPTER 5

Preinduction Visit
and Suggestibility Tests

—■—

The preinduction visit is the portion of time during the initial meeting with the patient that is used to explain what hypnosis is, what it is not and how hypnosis works. The following protocol has proven to be effective for childbirth, anaesthesia and pain management patients.

Preinduction Protocol

1. Explain what hypnosis is. Two basic definitions you may wish to use are:

    Hypnosis is an artificially induced state, usually (though not always) resembling sleep, but physiologically distinct from it, which is characterized by heightened suggestibility, as a result of which certain sensory, motor and memory abnormalities may be induced more readily than in the normal state. (Warren's Dictionary of Psychology).

    In a hypnotic state the body is a robot controlled by the mind. What the mind perceives or imagines as reality, the body must do and accept as reality. (R.D. Longacre, Ph.D.).

2. Explain what hypnosis is not.

    Hypnosis is not physical sleep. Hypnosis is not a state of unconsciousness. Hypnosis is not being gullible. Hypnosis is not being weak minded. Hypnosis is not being controlled by someone else. Hypnosis is not a loss of self-control. Hypnosis is not divulging secrets. No one can be hypnotized against their will or do anything in a state of hypnosis that violates their moral, religious or personal principles.

3. Demonstrate to the patient what hypnosis feels like.

Ask the patient to put their feet flat on the floor, heel to heel and toe to toe. Suggest that they place their arms so that their hands are resting comfortably on their lap. Ask them to take a few deep breaths and as they exhale, concentrate on the feeling of relaxation in the chest area. Now ask them to close their eyes and feel themselves relaxing more and more with each breath. Explain that as they continue to relax they are experiencing what hypnosis feels like.

Suggest that they concentrate on your voice and ignore all the other sounds they may hear. Suggest that they can go even deeper relaxed as you count back from three to one. On the number one tell them to open their eyes, stand up and hit their head against the nearest wall.

Obviously the patient will not follow this suggestion and most likely will be amused. Explain that they were experiencing what hypnosis feels like and that this structured exercise demonstrated that even in a state of hypnosis they are always in complete control. In other words, they will accept only the suggestions that are helpful to them and in their best interest.

4. Dispel the myths about stage hypnosis.

Explain that the people who volunteer to be a part of a stage hypnotism react as they do because they are looking for a good time. A hypnotic state enables them to release inhibitions much the same as social drinking or a party situation where they feel comfortable and relaxed.

Explain that these volunteers appear to be sleeping but they are not asleep and in fact are very aware of everything going on around them and their own reaction to suggestions given by the stage hypnotist.

If you ask people who agreed to be a part of a stage hypnosis show why they acted foolish or carried out a suggestion given by the stage hypnotist, they usually reply, "I was enjoying myself, having a good time" or "I knew what I was doing but I didn't see any reason for not going along with the fun."

5. Give a simple explanation of how therapeutic hypnosis works and why it is different from stage hypnosis.

    Explain that there is no room for theatrics in clinical hypno-therapy and that the patient will not be asked to do anything that is funny, humiliating or embarrassing. Provide the patient with an easily understood explanation of why therapeutic hypnosis works.

6. Demonstrate clinical hypnotic phenomena to the patient by conducting various suggestibility tests. It is important to remember that suggestibility tests provide an indication of the patient's ability to accept ideas, however, the main purpose of these tests is to establish a spiral of belief that enhances the patient's expectation of positive results.

Suggestibility Tests

There are many suggestibility tests that may be employed to enhance the patient's expectation of positive results with hypnotherapy and guided imagery. The suggestibility tests presented in this chapter provide the therapist a quantitative evaluation of the patient's ability to accept visual, auditory and kinesthetic suggestions as well as reinforcing the patient's expectation of positive results from therapy.

Suggestibility tests that are effective for therapists working in the area of hypnotic childbirth, anaesthesia and pain management include the sway test, the arm levitation test, the finger in a vice test and the lemon test.

The sway test will always provide positive results if the therapist observes the patient closely and paces his or her comments to match the patient's reaction to the suggestions that are given.

To perform this test, have the patient stand in front of you and place their feet next to each other, heel to heel and toe to toe. Ask the patient to let their arms relax and assume a vertical position alongside their body. Instruct the patient to keep their head erect as they look at an imaginary spot directly in front of them

Now ask the patient to look up without moving their head to an imaginary spot way above their head. You may wish to assist them by having them concentrate on an object you are holding in your hand and then raising the object to a point above their head. When they are focusing the pupils of their eyes on a real or imagined spot above their head, suggest that they close their eyes.

When the patient has closed their eyes, suggest that they will soon begin to sway as they concentrate on your voice. Suggest that may sway forward or backwards. Look for the patient's first movement (backwards or forwards) and then reinforce with appropriate suggestions, i.e., "You are swaying forward, now (watch for movement) you are swaying backward." Once the patient has established a rhythm and is following your suggestions, tell them that as they come forward they will continue to fall until you stop them.

Prevent the patient from actually falling by putting your hands on the front of their shoulders as they come toward you. Suggest that you will count from one to three and on the numeral three their eyes will open and they will feel normal in every way. Explain to the patient that this test demonstrates their ability to accept suggestions in a very light stage of hypnosis.

The arm levitation test also demonstrates the patient's ability to accept suggestions in a light stage of hypnosis.

To perform the arm levitation test, ask the patient to stand or sit in a chair, holding their head erect and concentrate on an imaginary spot directly in front of them. Instruct the patient to take a few deep lung filling breaths and concentrate on the feeling of relaxation in their chest area as they exhale. Now ask the patient to continue breathing deeply and close their eyes. Once they have closed their eyes, instruct them to raise their arms to a horizontal position or straight out in front of their body.

Most patients will raise one arm slightly higher than the other. If this is not the case give the following instructions before proceeding with the test.

Ask the patient to turn the thumb up on the right hand and the palm down on the left hand. This will cause one hand to be positioned lower than the other.

Now suggest that the lower arm is starting to become heavy and you are placing a very thick large black dictionary on the top of their hand. Touch the top of the hand you are placing the dictionary on and suggest that the dictionary is now making the arm very tired and it is slowly drifting down lower and lower toward the lap as the weight of the extremely heavy dictionary seems to push the arm down towards their lap.

Next suggest that you are placing a loop of string around the wrist of the other hand (lightly lift the hand) and the loop of string is tied to a large helium balloon. Tell the patient that the balloon is floating up towards the ceiling and the hand is becoming lighter and even lighter as the balloon gently lifts the hand higher and higher.

Alternate these two suggestions until maximal arm separation is observed. Now ask the patient to open their eyes.

Explain to the patient that in reality there is no dictionary or balloon but their subconscious mind accepted the suggestions and caused their body to react to a heavy dictionary and a balloon. This structured exercise demonstrates that whatever the mind accepts or perceives as reality, the body must do.

The finger in a vice test is an example of hypnosis with the eyes wide open. Test results are not as predictable as the sway test and arm levitation test. However, the appropriate explanation of test results can facilitate the patient's expectation and belief in their ability to accept suggestions and benefit from hypnotherapy.

To perform this test, have the patient sit comfortably in a chair and loosely clasp their hands. Have them straighten out the two pointer fingers so that they are opposite each other and slightly separated. Ask them to concentrate on the pointer fingers and take several deep relaxing breaths. Now suggest that as they concentrate on your voice, each deep lung filling breath will relax them deeper and even deeper. Have the patient continue to concentrate or stare at the pointer fingers as you demonstrate visually and comment on an imaginary vise or "C clamp" that you are placing around the fingers. As you turn the handle on this make believe vise, comment on the pressure the vice is applying to the fingers. This pressure is pushing the fingers tighter together, moving them together. Continue suggestions that the vice is pushing the fingers closer and closer to each other and the pressure causing this to happen is becoming greater and greater. Turn the imaginary handle until the fingers come together and reinforce with appropriate comments about seeing, feeling and imagining the vice closing tighter and tighter.

If the patient is not experiencing the pressure of the vice or is resistant to your suggestions tell them that this demonstrates the fact that they are in complete control of their thoughts and will accept your suggestions only if they really want to.

If the patient has accepted your suggestions compliment them on their ability to use their subconscious mind to instigate physiological body responses. Their ability to do this enhances the therapeutic goal they have expressed during the clinical interview.

The lemon test demonstrates the body is a robot theory and always has positive results unless the patient is recalcitrant or participating in the test in order to please you or another interested party.

To perform the lemon test, have the patient hold out their hand and concentrate on an imaginary lemon. Ask them to visualize and feel the imaginary lemon in the palm of their hand. Use guided imagery to help them imagine the lemon. Your imagery suggestions should appeal to as many of the five senses as possible.

Ask the patient to continue to picture and imagine the lemon as you count from one to three. Instruct the patient to lift their hand to their mouth and take a big bite out of the lemon on the numeral three. Reinforce the imagery of the lemon as you count slowly from one to three and on the numeral three tell them to put their hand to their mouth and take a big bite.

After biting into the lemon, the patient should experience a degree of salivation. They may even sense a sour or bitter taste when imagining biting into the lemon.

This test demonstrates that the patient's mind accepted the idea of biting into a lemon and their mind triggered a physiological response. In other words, their mouth became moist as it would when biting into a real lemon. The ability of the mind to trigger a physical response will serve them well when they wish to alleviate or ameliorate pain associated with childbirth, dental or surgical procedures or pain that is interfering with their quality of life.

CHAPTER 6

The Induction of Hypnosis

There are many methods that can be used to induce a state of therapeutic hypnosis. The progressive relaxation method is presented in this chapter because it can easily be modified to facilitate misdirected attention and increased concentration for a wide variety of patients or clients.

The progressive relaxation induction can combine both an authoritative and permissive approach with neurolinguistic imagery that enhances hypnotic relaxation for the individual patient or client.

Before beginning a progressive relaxation induction, have the patient sit comfortably in a chair with their feet flat on the floor. Have them position their arms alongside their body and place their hands on their lap. If the patient's physical condition or circumstances precludes sitting in a chair, place them in a high Fowler's or semi-Fowler's position.

The patient should be comfortable during the induction of hypnosis and not experience unnecessary weight or pressure on body areas that might inhibit circulation.

Patient comfort can be enhanced by making sure that their head and neck are gently supported with a pillow or high backed chair. Their feet should be flat on the floor with the legs uncrossed or slightly elevated and supported with a foot stool or pillow.

Voice tonality and tempo are important aspects of the progressive relaxation induction.

The tonality of voice must be soothing and calm. A sound of quiet confidence should instill a desire for complete relaxation on the part of the patient. The tempo of your voice should match the soothing rhythm of a lullaby or a parent comforting a small child.

The following script is intended to help you perfect a hypnotic relaxation technique. Practice reading the script in phrases rather than word by word. The dots between words indicate a relative pause between words or phrases. The italicized words should be spoken in a drawn out or elongated manner.

If you make a mistake when reading the script, do not stop or back up to the beginning. Assume you are giving suggestions to an actual patient or client, and keep on going. The imagery in the script follows a top of the head to the bottom of the foot progression.

Progressive Relaxation Script

Relax . . . just let yourself . . . relax . . . take a deep breath and let it out . . . *slowly* . . . Close your eyes and breathe . . . slowly and . . . *deeply* . . . Each time you exhale . . . I want you to feel all the tension leaving the chest area . . . In just a few moments you are going to be more relaxed than you have ever known yourself to be . . . I am going to mention different parts of your body . . . and as I do . . . I want you to feel that part . . . slowly begin to *relax* . . . Just let that part *slowly begin to relax.*

Beginning with the top of your head . . . I want you to imagine all the tiny little muscles and nerves on the top of the head . . . *relaxing* . . . and as each and every tissue and fiber relaxes . . . the wonderful feeling of *relaxation* . . . goes down from the head deeper and even deeper.

And as you relax deeper and . . . *even deeper* that warm wonderful feeling of relaxation begins to spread . . . from the top of your head to your forehead . . . and the forehead begins to *relax* and continuing to go deeper and even *deeper,* feel all the little worry lines in the forehead smoothing out and this warm feeling of relaxation goes even deeper down to the area around the eyes. And now the eyelids seem to become very . . . very *heavy* . . . They may want to flutter a little . . . that's OK . . . just feel how *heavy* they are.

This wonderful feeling of relaxation goes down to all the tiny little muscles in the facial area now . . . all the muscles in the facial area . . . just seem to . . . *relax*

. . . relaxing more and more . . . so that the jaw bone becomes heavy . . . the teeth may even part . . . The mouth may open a little as you go deeper and *deeper* relaxed. And you are so comfortable . . . so peaceful . . .

Now allow yourself . . . let yourself relax even deeper and the relaxation spreads to the area behind the ears . . . and going even deeper feel the relaxation coming to the back of the neck . . . and out into the shoulders . . . so much tension just seems to go out of the shoulders . . . they may even drop a little . . . And relaxing more and more now as this warm sense of relaxation spreads to the spinal column . . . and down the spinal column to the small of the back . . . And as you go even deeper relaxed . . . every muscle . . . every nerve and fiber in the back relaxes more and more . . .

And the relaxation continues even deeper . . . down over the buttocks and into the back of the thighs . . . down to the hollow of the knees . . . and even deeper to the calf of the legs . . . and farther down to the heel of the foot . . . across the bottom of the foot . . . and out into each and every toe . . . as you relax deeper and even *deeper* . . .

I am going to proceed to relax the rest of you now . . . beginning with the throat muscles . . . Feel all the throat muscles start to relax . . . and as you go deeper and even deeper . . . this wonderful sense of relaxation goes down to the front of the shoulders . . . down into the upper arms . . . deeper down over the elbow . . . into the forearms . . . down the wrists . . . out into the hands and deeper down to the tip of each and every finger . . . The fingers may even want to move a little as you go deeper and even deeper relaxed . . .

Now concentrate on the throat area again . . . every muscle and nerve ending so very relaxed . . . and with each lung filling, relaxing breath you go deeper and even deeper relaxed . . . And the relaxation continues deeper down into the chest area . . . down into the abdomen . . . and all the muscles in the chest and stomach area relax more and even more . . . And the relaxation goes deeper down now . . . to the front of the thighs . . . down over the knees . . . down the shin bone . . . into the instep of the foot . . . across the top of the foot . . . and into each and every toe . . .

So very calm and peaceful now . . . every part of your body so totally and completely relaxed . . . More relaxed than you have ever known yourself to be . . .

The patient should now be in a light state of hypnosis. Before proceeding with therapeutic suggestions, a basic deepening technique is indicated.

The following script is suggested as a basic technique for behavior modification therapy as well as hypnotic anaesthesia. Advanced deepening techniques for anaesthesia will be presented in the chapter on hypnotic childbirth.

A Basic Deepening Technique

I want you to picture and imagine now . . . that you and I are standing at the top of a flight of ten beautiful stairs . . . We are going to go down these stairs together and as we do you will be able to go deeper and even . . . deeper relaxed . . . is that OK with you . . . nod your head please . . . very well . . .

Picture and imagine you and I at the top of the stairs . . . These stairs are covered in your favorite color of carpet . . . I am going to count from ten down to zero as we walk down these stairs together . . . Each numeral will take you deeper down . . . relaxed . . . so peaceful and so very . . . very . . . comfortable . . . relaxed . . . On the numeral zero you will enter a beautiful place of peace and tranquility called deep . . . deep . . . relaxation . . . Is that OK with you . . . nod your head please . . .

Very well . . . take that first step down . . . ten . . . deeper down . . . nine . . . and deeper . . . eight . . . deeper . . . seven . . . and even deeper . . . six . . . five . . . and deeper . . . four . . . three . . . all the way down now . . . two . . . way down . . . one . . . On the next numeral you will enter this beautiful place of peace . . . comfort and tranquility . . . called . . . deep . . . deep relaxation . . . is that alright with you . . . All the way down now . . . zero.

The patient should now be ready to accept therapeutic suggestions and act upon suggestions that they find reasonable, acceptable and in their best interest.

CHAPTER 7

Therapeutic Suggestion Formulation

---◼---

The Psychology of Suggestions

A suggestion is any single thought, series of thoughts, ideas, words, beliefs or actions given in any manner. Suggestions can be direct, indirect, conscious, subconscious or unconscious that change or alter a person's normal behavior pattern.

Understanding the psychology of suggestions will enable the hypnotherapist to develop guided imagery that is effective for hypnotic childbirth, anaesthesia and pain management patients.

Therapeutic suggestions instigate a psychological process that produces a physiological result. Therapeutic suggestions may also be defined as any process whereby a person accepts a command, plea, proposition, thought, idea, belief or any direction to be acted upon, in the absence of any critical or reflective thoughts which would normally occur.

Before formulating suggestions for individual patients or clients, the therapist must understand specific types of suggestions and the "Hypnotic Formula."

The hypnotic formula equates expectation, suggestions and imagination and the interaction of these components that facilitate a state of hypnosis.

The hypnotic formula states that hypnosis equals expectation, catalyzed by imagination that produces belief which in turn leads to conviction and desired therapeutic results.

Hypnosis = Expectation + Imagination = Belief
Therefore
Belief = Conviction + Expectation = Hypnosis

A therapeutic suggestion does not produce hypnosis. Imagination does not produce hypnosis. Suggestions must stimulate imagination to produce a state of hypnosis and resultant therapeutic results.

Therapeutic suggestions should be given to the patient in a manner that enables them to expect a desired outcome and enables them to use their imagination to produce the results they desire.

Therapeutic suggestions should begin with simple statements that predispose positive results during suggestibility tests. Positive results from suggestibility tests enhance the patient's belief and conviction and stimulate their imagination.

The patient's ability to picture and imagine fosters belief and conviction that future clinical suggestions will be accepted by their subconscious and produce the desired therapeutic results.

If the above seems a bit confusing, stop for a moment and consider how suggestions have influenced your life from the day you were born.

The following types of suggestions may have had an influence on your behavior.

Direct	Hetero
Indirect	Waking
Inferred	Specific
Prestige	Non-prestige
Unconscious	Blanket
Auto	Post-hypnotic
Negative	Positive

Direct Suggestions

A direct suggestion is any verbal statement or physical action that is direct, to the point and without camouflage and is given in an "Authoritative" or "Persuasive" manner.

Some examples of direct suggestions are; "Everybody stand up" (authoritative) "Everybody stand up please" (persuasive) "Come here" and "Eat your food."

Indirect Or Inferred Suggestions

Indirect or inferred suggestions are not generally recognized as suggestions because they are primarily nonverbal motions or sounds. The subject is usually not aware of the influence of this type of suggestion on his or her normal behavior pattern.

Some examples of indirect suggestions are; cough and you cause others to cough, yawn and you cause others to yawn, smile and you cause others to smile and if you show fear or anger those around you tend to respond in a like manner.

Prestige Suggestions

Prestige suggestions are those that you accept and act upon without second thought or contradiction, because they were given by a person of prestige who you like, trust, respect or have a great degree of confidence in.

People who are associated with prestige suggestions enhance your quality of life or health. These people include; doctors, nurses, dentists, psychologists, teachers, clergy, lawyers, entertainers, friends, parents and relatives.

Non Prestige Suggestions

Non-prestige suggestions influence people who are alert but may not be aware of their psychological or physiological responses to this type of suggestion.

Examples of non-prestige suggestions are; music that suggests happiness, sadness, romance, tranquility or other emotions. The sight or smell of food may suggest hunger. The sight or sound of rain may suggest freshness, cleanliness, coziness or depression.

Unconscious Suggestions

Unconscious suggestions are comments, statements or stimuli accepted by a person who is in a highly receptive state such as hypnosis or under the influence of chemical anaesthesia.

Auto Suggestions

Auto-suggestions are thoughts or ideas that a person gives to themselves in a wake state or in a meditative, alpha or hypnotic state.

Hetero Suggestions

Hetero suggestions are given by one person to another person.

Post Hypnotic Suggestions

Post hypnotic suggestions are given by a therapist to a patient or client to instigate a therapeutic behavior after the patient or client has been dehypnotized.

Negative Suggestions

Negative suggestions are those that intentionally or unintentionally produce a state of tension, stress, anxiety, fear or confusion. Negative suggestions can be externally induced or implanted by a given individual.

Negative suggestions are destructive and cause a lack of self-confidence and esteem. Negative suggestions can be accepted or acted upon on a conscious or a subconscious level.

Some examples of negative suggestions are; "You can't make it in this world unless you are rich," "What's the use, nobody cares anyway," "It's not what you know it's who you know" and "You just can't win no matter how hard you try."

Examples of negative suggestions that produce physical manifestations include; "I get sick to my stomach every time I think about it," "My job gives me a pain in the neck," "I can't sleep at night because my job is driving me crazy" and "One more day like this and I think I'm going to die."

A negative suggestion can also be a simple word such as *try* or *maybe*. The word *try* suggests that maybe I will and maybe I won't. *Maybe* is a word that allows us to put off taking responsibility for a positive expectation. Other negative words include; *hope, I think, wish, never, can't, sometimes* and *won't*.

Therapeutic suggestions must be formulated so that they do not contain negative words, expressions or suggestions. Positive suggestions and end result imagery enable the patient to achieve the therapeutic results they desire.

Positive Suggestions

Positive suggestions are those that produce self-confidence, self-esteem, inner strength and direction. Positive suggestions also produce a sense of purpose and "feeling good" emotions like happiness and calmness.

Formulating Therapeutic Suggestions

There are two basic types of suggestions that are used during hypnotherapy. These suggestions can be classified as direct (specific) and inferred (blanket).

Direct or specific suggestions are used to establish a purpose, direction or goal. An example of a direct suggestion is "As soon as you sit in the dental chair you are closing your eyes and with each deep lung filling breath, you are relaxing deeper and deeper, as deeply relaxed as you are now in this chair."

Inferred or blanket suggestions are used to release or trade off any past experience that may be a contributing factor to a current unwanted behavior. An example of an inferred suggestions is, "With each deep lung filling breath you feel the relaxation in the chest area and all the tension, stress and anxiety just seems to float away from your body like a tiny twig or leaf floating away in a fresh spring breeze."

The formulation of effective therapeutic suggestions affects the positive outcome of hypnotherapy more than the induction technique or awakening procedure.

When formulating therapeutic suggestions, it is important to remember that only the conscious mind reacts to logical, analytical or sequential thought processes. Abstract thoughts, memory and suggestions given in hypnotherapy are acted upon by the subconscious mind.

Since past conditioning, experiences and subsequent beliefs are anchored in the subconscious, therapeutic suggestions must be given in a positive manner and worded so that the suggestions can be accepted and acted upon by the subconscious mind.

Summary

Avoid negative words and phrases when formulating therapeutic suggestions.

Wrong
I will and I must have a better memory.
I will try to lose five pounds this month.
I must try to stop smoking.

Right
I am confident in my ability to recall all the information I have stored in my memory banks.

I am thinking thin and eating only the amount of food I know is necessary to maintain my good health.

I am a non-smoker and enjoying life more and more each day.

Try and *lose* are negative words that presuppose self-doubt and allow the individual a choice and a way out. Losing means that one searches for that which is lost, until it is found or replaced by another habit, feeling or emotion. Words like "I will" or "I must" are seldom accepted or acted upon by the subconscious.

Hypnotherapists must formulate suggestions so that they give the patient confidence, belief and expectation that their desired goal will happen.

Suggestions should be formulated so that they cover a wide area of possible results from therapy. Suggestions should paint word pictures and appeal to as many of the five senses as possible.

To insure optimal therapeutic results, suggestions should combine both an authoritative and permissive approach.

CHAPTER 8

The Awakening Procedure

Before beginning an awakening procedure, it is wise to suggest to the patient some type of simple task that will demonstrate to them that they were in a state of hypnosis when therapeutic suggestions were given. These simple tasks are often referred to as convincers. A convincer enables the patient to logically realize in the wake state that therapeutic suggestions are implanted in the subconscious mind and that they will be able to use these suggestions to achieve their desired goal.

I have found that most patients will insist they were not in a state of hypnosis and express a minimal belief in positive results unless they can be convinced that they were in fact hypnotized.

In my practice, the following convincers have been beneficial for a majority of patients and enhance conviction and belief in the positive results of hypnotherapy.

Convincers

1. Your eyelids are so heavy now that you cannot open them. The more you try to open them the heavier they become. Try to open your eyelids and the more you try the heavier they become.

2. Your left hand is so heavy it seems to be stuck or glued to your lap. The more you try to lift your hand the heavier it becomes. Try to lift it and it becomes so heavy even you cannot lift it.

3. A post hypnotic suggestion may also be given as a convincer. An example is, when you awaken you will find the chair you are sitting in so uncomfortable that you can no longer sit in it. The only way you can make the chair comfortable is to stand up. As soon as you stand up you will

find the chair to be the most comfortable chair you have ever sat in.

If a post hypnotic suggestion is given to demonstrate to the patient that they were hypnotized, be sure to remove the suggestion before ending the therapy session.

Awakening

One of the most ambiguous myths about hypnosis is the danger associated with the therapist not being able to awaken the subject.

The hypnotherapist does not need extensive training or experience to alert or awaken a patient.

It is a fact . . . If the therapist merely says "awake," the patient will eventually awake from the hypnotic state. This method is not advised and is strongly contraindicated for hypnotic anaesthesia patients or clients.

It is a fact . . . If the therapist leaves the room and does not return while the patient is experiencing hypnotic sleep, the patient will automatically slip into normal or physiological sleep and awaken after enjoying a refreshing nap.

The awakening procedure is used to avoid frightening the patient during dehypnotization. A patient that is gruffly awakened from hypnotic sleep could be startled into a state of hysteria.

The amount of time used to awaken or alert a patient should be equivalent to the amount of time devoted to inducing hypnosis. This rule of thumb does not apply when using the Progressive Relaxation method of induction.

When awakening or alerting a patient, always treat their ego with dignity and respect. Words and phrases used during the awakening procedure should reflect empathy and kindliness. Awakening suggestions should be thorough and complete. Awakening suggestions should enable the patient to feel refreshed, enthused about changes they wish to make in their lives and prevent iatrogenic complications.

It is recommended that the therapist condition the patient for rapid induction of hypnosis during the awakening procedure. Rapid reinduction of hypnosis is indicated if more than two therapy sessions are required to help the patient with their presenting complaint or problem.

The therapist should also guard the client from rehypnotization by a poorly trained or "Johnny come lately" hypnotist. The professional therapist should suggest that the patient must give their permission to be hypnotized and then they must be in an appropriate place at an appropriate time before they can experience the relaxing and comfortable feeling of hypnosis.

Therapeutic suggestions given during the awakening procedure should be presented in a bright and enthusiastic manner. Voice tonality should be confident and assertive. Post hypnotic suggestions may be repeated during the awakening procedure.

The following awakening script incorporates the precautions and special considerations for awakening or alerting a patient.

Awakening Script

I am going to count from one to ten . . . and as I do you will awaken slowly . . . As I count, each number will awaken you a little more. When I say the number seven you will be wide awake and feeling a wonderful glow of health and a sense of well being . . . and enjoying this and every day of your life . . .

You can relax as deeply as you are now any time you desire to do so . . . When you want to experience this warm comforting relaxation all you have to do is give your permission to a professional therapist or to yourself . . . Is that OK with you . . . nod your head please . . . very well . . . When you give your permission you will be able to instantly relax as deep as you are now . . . I am going to count now from one to ten . . .

One . . . two . . . (reinforce post hypnotic suggestions if desired) slowly coming up . . . Three . . . Four . . . coming up more and more . . . five . . . coming way up now . . . Six

. . . and enjoying a wonderful sense of well being . . . normal in every way . . . And Seven . . . eyes open wide awake . . . Eight . . . Feeling wonderful . . . refreshed. . . normal in every way . . . Nine and Ten . . . eyes open wide awake.

This awakening procedure was designed for patients or clients who were in a light to medium stage of hypnosis. If a patient has been guided into a deep level of hypnosis for anaesthesia, the awakening procedure presented in the chapter on hypnotic anaesthesia should be used.

Many times a patient will enjoy the feeling of deep relaxation so much that they will resist the awakening procedure. If the patient appears to ignore your suggestions to awaken, repeat the awakening suggestions in a loud voice. Voice inflection and tonality should be authoritative and firm when repeating these suggestions.

CHAPTER 9

Hypnotic Natural Childbirth

The use of hypnosis during labor and delivery can enable the mother to relax more completely than any other natural childbirth method. However, it is recommended that hypnosis be used as an adjunct to the various prepared childbirth techniques.

In order to obtain the optimum results and therapeutic objectives of hypnotic childbirth, the patient should be well-trained in using self-hypnosis and participate in a professionally recognized childbirth education class.

Indications

1. Reduction or eradication of fear, tension and pain before, during and after labor and delivery with a resultant elevation of the pain threshold.

2. Reduction of the amount of pain medication required to maintain the patient's comfort.

3. Patient control of painful uterine contractions which may be experienced during normal labor and delivery.

4. Decreased shock and speedier recovery.

5. Amelioration of undesirable post operative effects.

6. Hypnosis shortens the first stage of labor by approximately three to four hours for mothers who are experiencing labor and delivery for the first time.

7. Hypnosis raises resistance to fatigue concomitant with arduous or prolonged labor. Therefore maternal exhaustion can be alleviated and mothers can be more alert and aware when their baby is born.

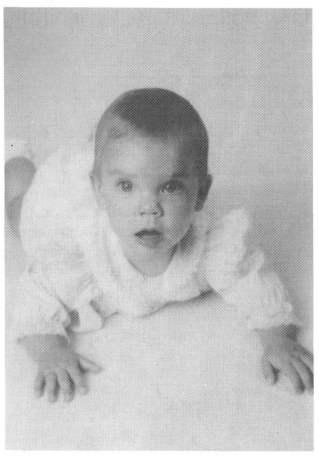

I recommend hypnotic childbirth for mothers, and fathers and new babies.

8. Hypnotic rapport can be transferred to a nurse, associate, husband or childbirth coach. Individuals participating in the birthing process do not need special training to assist the patient using self-hypnosis.

Hypnotic natural childbirth is an intensely gratifying experience for well-adjusted mothers. Hearing baby's first cry, seeing their newborn child and holding their baby in the delivery room may not be as joyful for mothers who are heavily sedated or exhausted from the work of labor.

Contraindications

There is no possibility that harm will be done to the mother or baby when self-hypnosis is used for anaesthesia. However, the literature does offer considerable evidence that when drugs are given for the relief of pain during childbirth, they may decrease the oxygen supply to the fetus.

A decreased amount of oxygen being supplied to the unborn baby through the placental membrane or decreased amounts of oxygen due to asphyxial factors such as trauma or difficult delivery, may produce fetal anoxia. Fetal anoxia may cause severe brain damage. The danger of fetal anoxia may be markedly decreased when the mother is using self-hypnosis techniques during childbirth.

Precautions

When working with patients who are using self-hypnosis for labor and delivery, the health care provider should remember that the patient is in a heightened state of awareness and suggestibility.

When communicating with the patient, the following words and phrases should be avoided; Labor pains, Pain medication, This will hurt a little, and Are your pains getting worse.

Preferred words and phrases are positive and enhance patient relaxation. Some examples are; Let yourself relax deeper with each contraction, Are your contractions getting closer? With each contraction imagine yourself drifting deeper down, deeper relaxed, and allow yourself to relax even deeper as I give you medication to help you with the work of childbirth.

The use of self-hypnosis does not negate the need for necessary pain medication. Pain medication should be readily available for the patient. Only one in four mothers have the ability to forego analgesia completely during labor and delivery.

All childbirth patients should be informed that pain medication is available upon request. The patient should also be assured that they need not feel guilty when requesting medication to help them maintain comfort during the birthing process.

Hypnotic childbirth patients should also understand that it is not necessary for them to go through the entire birthing process in a state of hypnosis. Explain to the patient that they can alert themselves and experience the work of labor whenever they want to.

The goal or purpose of self-hypnosis and deep relaxation during childbirth is to minimize unnecessary pain or discomfort for the mother, not to eliminate or circumvent traditional medical care and treatment.

Hypnotic Childbirth Instruction

Preconditioning for hypnotic childbirth should begin during the third or fourth month of pregnancy The number of sessions required to teach the patient self-hypnosis techniques may vary from one to twenty. Six training sessions, prior to the patient's presentation for childbirth, are usually sufficient to insure a rewarding birthing experience.

Regardless of the number of self-hypnosis training sessions, the therapist should emphasize that the patient does not need to experience any more discomfort than she is willing to bear. Before terminating training sessions, the therapist should assess the patient's ability to achieve a medium stage of hypnosis quickly and easily.

The clinical application of glove anaesthesia and techniques to instruct a patient in this hypnotherapeutic modality are discussed in the chapter on hypnotic anaesthesia.

The following instructional program is generally effective for a majority of hypnotic childbirth patients.

Six-Session Protocol

Session Number One

During the first session have the patient read informational material about hypnosis and hypnotic natural childbirth. The patient should then fill out a standard intake form.

The intake form should provide you with information regarding any potential problems that may arise during therapy. This form should contain information about the patient's primary physician and attending OB/GYN.

The patient's OB/GYN should be advised about his patient's desire for hypnotherapy for childbirth and be informed that you will send him progress reports and an evaluation of therapeutic results for his records. Most physicians seldom object to hypnotherapy for childbirth and are willing to work with the therapist to insure maximal results for the patient.

When the patient has read the informational material and completed the intake form, they should listen to a patient education cassette on hypnotic natural childbirth. The cassette should include information about what hypnosis feels like, what the patient can expect during labor and delivery and a brief account of the personal experience of a mother who used hypnotic childbirth techniques. Patient expectation of positive results from therapy is enhanced if this cassette features a specialist in hypnotic anaesthesia or childbirth and the voice of a mother who had a joyful birthing experience using self-hypnosis.

The hypnotic childbirth therapist should review the intake form, conduct a clinical interview, perform suggestibility tests and place the patient in a light stage of hypnosis.

Therapeutic suggestions given during the first session should be formulated to instill confidence that childbirth will be a normal and natural body process and a joyful experience for the mother-to-be. Suggestions should also be given to demonstrate glove anaesthesia to the patient and to demonstrate the depth of hypnosis achieved during the first visit.

You can demonstrate to the patient the depth of hypnosis they were able to reach during the first session by using a technique referred to as Dr. Longacre's Hypnodepthmeter. This technique suggests that the patient picture and imagine a yardstick with large easy to read numbers and an arrow that can move up and down the yardstick. The number the arrow is pointing to is an indication of the patient's level of hypnosis. The following imagery script is recommended when using the hypnodepthmeter to determine the patient's level of hypnosis or when using Dr. Longacre's technique to deepen the hypnotic state.

Dr. Longacre's Hypnodepthmeter

Now I want you to picture and imagine that there is a yardstick leaning against a wall. The yardstick has large easy to read numbers. The number 36 is at the top of the yardstick and the number 1 is at the bottom of the yardstick. Concentrate on the yardstick with your mind's eye. Now picture and imagine that a large arrow is pointing to a number on the yardstick. The arrow can point to any number you choose.

The numbers on the yardstick have special meaning and are personal numbers for you. If the arrow is pointing at numbers from 36 down to 25, it means you are in a light state of comfortable hypnosis. If the arrow points to the numbers 24 down to 13, it means you are in a medium, very relaxed and comfortable state of hypnosis and if the arrow points to numbers from 12 down to 1, it means you are in a very relaxed, tranquil, comfortable and enjoyable state of hypnosis.

With your mind's eye, imagine the yardstick and the arrow. When I ask you what number the arrow is pointing to, you will be able to tell me the number you see, imagine or feel and remain deeply relaxed and comfortable. Concentrate on the number the arrow is pointing to and when you know the number, nod your head please. Very well, what number is the arrow pointing to.

When the hypnodepthmeter is used as a deepening technique, have the patient imagine that the arrow is sliding down the yardstick as you count from five to one and then ask them what number the arrow is pointing to. This can be repeated until they answer with a number below ten. If further deepening is desired, change the color of the arrow to blue and repeat the above suggestions elaborating on the increasing depth of hypnosis indicated by the numbers on the yardstick.

This technique can be repeated using a white arrow if the therapist wishes to induce a very deep state of hypnotic anaesthesia.

Hypnotic childbirth patients usually visualize or report a number indicative of a medium level of hypnosis during their first session. On their second visit the number should be lower and information solicited while they are practicing self-hypnosis.

Once the patient's initial level of hypnosis has been established, hypnotic natural childbirth therapy suggestions may be given.

Hypnotic Childbirth Imagery

After inducing a state of hypnosis and performing appropriate deepening techniques, continue with the following imagery script.

Now feel yourself relaxing deeper and even deeper . . . And as you go deeper and deeper relaxed you will be able to . . . picture and imagine the marvelous joy of childbirth . . . And you are enjoying every moment, so peaceful, so content, so very calm, tranquil . . . And you are recognizing and realizing how wonderful your birthing experience is for you and your baby.

And just relaxing deeper and even deeper feel how wonderful your birthing experience will be. Your baby in now within you developing and growing preparing for entry into this world. Let yourself, allow yourself to feel and imagine your baby smiling looking at you with love and adoration . . . Feel your baby snuggling in your arms . . . so content, soft looking into your eyes with love and adoration . . . You are a wonderful mother.

Your child's birth is going to be a completely and natural event in your life . . . Childbirth is a joyful experience and a perfectly natural process of your body and mind. Visualize and feel yourself relaxing during childbirth . . . So courageous, so confident. so strong and deeply relaxed.

Now imagine that you are giving birth to your baby . . . Realizing that you are not actually giving birth . . . just imagine how wonderful it will be. And one group of muscles in the womb relaxing so baby can go farther down . . . other muscles working to push baby out . . . And all the muscles working together in perfect harmony . . . easily and naturally.

See yourself feeling so very good . . . so healthy, strong, confident in your ability to give birth to a healthy baby full of peace, joy and relaxation. And you are recognizing and realizing that the work of childbirth will be as easy and natural as any other process of your body.

And as you go deeper and deeper relaxed you can imagine and hear your baby's first cry. You will be alert when your baby is born . . . you will be deeply relaxed and hear your baby's first cry . . . You are very relaxed . . . peaceful, calm and composed . . . And you are looking forward to the wonderful joy of giving birth.

I'm going to let you rest for a moment . . . relaxing deeper and even deeper . . . just relaxing and enjoying the warmth and love of your baby . . . See your baby's beautiful eyes . . . feel your baby's soft pink skin . . . And imagine your baby in your arms. You are a wonderful, loving and caring mother . . . A perfect mother in every way . . .

Before alerting or awakening the patient, give the appropriate suggestions to induce glove anaesthesia. Demonstrate the phenomena of glove anaesthesia to the patient. Glove anaesthesia is an excellent way to convince the patient that they were in fact hypnotized.

A post hypnotic suggestion is then given to reinforce the patient's ability to use an eye elevation focal point technique to rapidly induce self-hypnosis.

When using the focal point technique, the patient holds their head in an erect position and elevates the pupils of their eyes to a point high above their head. The patient concentrates on this imaginary focal point until they feel their eyelids tiring and becoming heavy. When the eyelids feel heavy, they suggest to themselves that as they count from three down to one, the eyelids will get heavier and on the numeral one the eyelids will close and they will be able to instantly drift down to the depth of hypnosis they are currently experiencing.

After alerting the patient, have them practice the eye elevation focal point technique. The hypnodepthmeter may be used to determine the patient's ability to induce an appropriate level of self-hypnosis.

Instruct the patient to practice this technique daily until their next therapy session.

Session Number Two

Begin the second session by testing the patient to determine their primary learning or information accessing system.

Include hypnosis by talking the patient through the focal point self-induction technique. Repeat the glove anaesthesia demonstration and hypnotic childbirth therapy suggestions.

Before you alert the patient, give post hypnotic suggestions that reinforce their ability to reach a nice state of deep relaxation using the focal point self-hypnosis technique.

Session Number Three

The husband or childbirth coach is asked to participate in the third session. Begin the session by having the patient practice self-induction and glove anaesthesia.

While the patient is in a hypnotic state, suggest that they can return to this state easily and instantly from the wake state when their birthing partner gently squeezes the patient's wrist with a finger and the thumb. This suggestion should be repeated with other appropriate post hypnotic suggestions.

After alerting the patient, have them work with their partner until they are able to employ the wrist squeeze technique as a method of rapid induction from the wake state.

Session Number Four

The patient's partner is encouraged to participate in the fourth visit session. Have the patient practice self-induction, glove anaesthesia and the wrist squeeze technique.

At the conclusion of the fourth session, give the patient printed information for her to present to hospital personnel assisting her in labor and delivery. This material should explain the indications and precautions for hypnotic natural childbirth and instructions for assisting patients who are using self-hypnosis during labor and delivery.

A childbirth reinforcement cassette is also given to the patient for home use. This tape should include a progressive relaxation induction and suggestions that enhance the results of individual therapy sessions.

Session Number Five

During the fifth session, all material and hypnotic childbirth techniques are reviewed. You should discuss any problems or questions the patient is having in therapy. Before concluding this session, you should ground the patient as to the appropriate place and time for using hypnosis.

Depending on the patient's preference, the appropriate place may be in her home, at a birthing center or in the hospital.

The appropriate time is usually when the patient reaches the place she has selected for childbirth.

By grounding the patient as to place and time, you enhance their expectation in positive results. Grounding the patient also prevents the possibility that they will use self-hypnosis to ignore the early signs of labor and have to unnecessarily rush to get to the hospital before the transitional stage of labor begins.

Session Number Six

The sixth session is devoted to practicing all the self-hypnosis skills that the patient has learned. Additional sessions may be scheduled at this time if further self-hypnosis training is requested by the patient or therapeutic goals have not been met.

Summary

If the patient or the hypnotherapist is experiencing any difficulty or problems during the course of hypnotic childbirth instruction, a consult with another childbirth professional is indicated. The patient may wish to consult their physician or prepared childbirth instructor. The therapist should consult a specialist in hypnotic childbirth who has been certified by the National Board for Hypnotic Anaesthesiology, or a physician with training in medical hypnosis.

The patient should be taught glove anaesthesia and rapid induction techniques or self-hypnosis. They should be able to demonstrate proficiency in using these techniques before completing a course of instruction in hypnotic childbirth.

The therapists should keep an open line of communication with other health care providers working with the expectant mother and provide written progress reports or a summary of therapeutic goals and results to primary physicians.

Management Of Labor With Hypnosis

The induction of labor can be facilitated with hypnosis. This is accomplished by regressing the patient to her last experience with labor and delivery and having her revivify all the subjective associations with the onset of labor.

Hypnosis can also help prevent undesired premature labor. Suggestions to retard premature labor should emphasize a normal and natural delivery and deep relaxation imagery. In other words, the deeper the mother is able to relax, the more the muscles used for childbirth will relax until it is time to begin the work of childbirth.

The patient can experience labor contractions as pressure rather then pain if she desires to do so. The three hypnotherapy modalities used to help the patient accomplish a painless childbirth experience are; misdirection of attention, the wrist squeeze maneuver and glove anaesthesia.

The misdirection of attention technique is used after the therapist has guided the patient into a light state of auto-hypnosis. The focal point method of self-hypnosis works quite nicely for most patients. As the therapist helps the patient with self-induction, the patient is asked to breathe deeply in the same manner in which they were trained in a parenting class.

When the patient has reached a light state of hypnosis, suggest that they can count the number of breaths during each contraction and remain very relaxed. The patient is then asked to total the number of breaths for two contractions and then divide this number by two. This is the average number of breaths per contraction. The patient should make a mental note of this average number and then repeat this procedure during the next two contractions and so on.

The therapist should now suggest that the patient will relax deeper and even deeper each time they keep track of the average number of breaths for each contraction and will recognize that the number of breaths decreases each time they count. This indicates that their labor is progressing nicely and that they are relaxing more and more.

The wrist squeeze maneuver allows the husband or coach to help the patient mitigate the sensation of pain in addition to helping the patient instantly deeply relax from the wake state. The husband or coach is instructed to gently squeeze the patient's wrist and suggest, "As the pressure on your wrist decreases you will be able to go deeper relaxed and feeling only pressure with each contraction." This suggestion should be repeated between labor contractions as well as during contractions.

The wrist squeeze maneuver can be practiced during hypnotic childbirth training sessions by having the patient's partner or coach gently squeeze the patient's wrist and repeat the following suggestions. "As I gently squeeze your wrist you are allowing yourself to go deeper and deeper relaxed. As I hold your wrist let yourself feel all the tension leaving the chest area as you breathe in deeply and exhale slowly. You are breathing in pure clean air and relaxation and as you exhale, all the tension is leaving your body. And as I release the pressure on your wrist you are instantly and easily relaxing deeper and faster."

When the therapist observes that the patient is apparently relaxing with this maneuver, they should suggest to the patient that this feeling of relaxation will occur every time the birthing partner squeezes their wrist. Tell the patient that if they are in the wake state, the wrist squeeze will enable them to instantly go into a hypnotic state for childbirth. If the patient is in a hypnotic state, they will go deeper relaxed and feel only pressure with each contraction.

The third technique that can be used during labor and delivery to alleviate unnecessary pain is glove anaesthesia. This technique is discussed in detail in the chapter on Hypnotic Anaesthesia.

Glove anaesthesia allows the patient to experience labor contractions as pressure when they place their hands on the abdominal area. This technique can also enable the patient to experience a feeling of numbness in the lower spine for relief of back labor. Glove anaesthesia can also be used during delivery and for postpartum discomfort.

Prior to delivery, glove anaesthesia can provide analgesia to the perineal area. Since only one in four patients will be able to achieve a total feeling of numbness, a local anaesthetic should be given prior to an episiotomy.

The glove anaesthesia technique along with end result imagery can alleviate the discomfort of post-partum contractions and enhance the healing of perineum tissue.

Other Clinical Applications Of Hypnosis

During the course of pregnancy, hypnosis can provide relief from the heartburn of pregnancy or hyperemesis gravidarum.

The literature reports two etiologies for hyperemesis gravidarum. One cause of this disorder is associated with toxemia, the other with stress, tension and various concurrent nervous disorders.

The treatment of toxic hyperemesis gravidarum (morning sickness) with hypnotherapy is contraindicated. Hyperemesis gravidarum that has a psychogenic basis can be alleviated with hypno-therapy.

Therapeutic suggestions for hyperemesis gravidarum should be directed toward the relief of tension and anxiety. Glove anaesthesia and self-hypnosis can also be employed to ameliorate this condition

Glove anaesthesia, safe place imagery and pain or anxiety as the object imagery may be employed to alleviate lower back and leg discomfort associated with physiological changes that take place during pregnancy. These changes include but are not limited to; change in posture, increased weight and inhibition of circulation to extremities due to the position of the fetus inside the mother's womb.

After delivery, lactation problems can be alleviated with hypnosis. Hypnotic suggestions that may enhance lactation should enable the patient to picture and imagine full breasts and milk flowing normally and naturally from the breasts to the baby.

CHAPTER 10

Hypnotic Anaesthesia

Hypnotic anaesthesia is indicated for alleviation of pain in the hospital setting, during dentistry and for patients suffering chronic pain for a variety of physiological or psychogenic disorders. Specific techniques for chronic pain management will be discussed in the chapter on Pain Management.

Clinical techniques used to induce hypnotic anaesthesia include; Dissociation, Disorientation and Glove Anaesthesia. These techniques are employed after a patient is placed in a state of hypnosis and a basic deepening technique has been suggested. The patient should be in a medium state of hypnosis before appropriate anaesthesia deepening suggestions are given by the therapist.

A standard deepening procedure that is effective for most patients is imagery that suggests they are walking down a flight of ten stairs. The therapist paints a word picture of the stairs and the room at the bottom of the stairs and then suggests that the patient can relax even deeper as they walk down this flight of stairs.

The following imagery script is suggested for this basic deepening technique: "Picture and imagine that you and I are standing at the top of a flight of ten beautiful stairs. These stairs are covered in your favorite color of carpet and feel very comfortable beneath your feet. We are going to walk down these stairs together, and as we do you will relax even deeper. With each numeral you will go deeper relaxed. Is that OK with you? Nod your head please, very well . . ."

The therapist now counts from ten down to zero and emphasizes that the patient is going deeper relaxed, drifting down, relaxing deeper and deeper, etc. Before saying the numeral zero, the therapist should suggest that on the numeral zero the patient will enter a beautiful place of peace, tranquility and deep relaxation, more relaxed than they have ever known themselves to be. The therapist should ask the patient if they want to enter this special place called deep hypnosis. If the patient's answer is affirmative, the therapist says the numeral zero.

Deepening Procedures

Deepening procedures that are generally effective for hypnotic anaesthesia patients are; Hand Rotation Procedure, Vogt's Fractionation and Dr. Longacre's Hypnodepthmeter.

Hand Rotation

To perform the hand rotation procedure, instruct the patient to slowly move their hands around one another. After this movement is well established, suggest to the patient that they can go deeper and even deeper and as they continue to relax, their hands will move faster and faster.

Observe the patient's hand movement and continue to suggest that they are going deeper and their hands are rotating faster and faster. When an accelerated rate of hand rotation is observed, tell the patient to stop moving their hands and place them comfortably on their lap. Suggest that when their hands touch their lap, they will go even deeper relaxed. Reassure the patient throughout the deepening procedure. Explain to them that they are doing well and relaxing easily and naturally.

This technique is particularly effective for a patient who has not been able to achieve a deep state of hypnosis during previous therapy. To insure optimum results, have the patient observe another subject who is capable of deepening hypnosis with the hand rotation procedure before beginning therapy.

Vogt's Fractionation

Vogt's Fractionation procedure feeds back thoughts and sensations the patient experienced while in a previous state of hypnosis. The therapist suggests to the patient that as they remember these feelings and thoughts, they will relax faster and deeper.

To use this procedure, place the patient in a state of hypnosis and before dehypnotization ask them to relate feelings, thoughts, colors or other sensations they experienced during the trance. After soliciting this information, suggest to the patient that they will be able to achieve a deeper level of hypnosis each time they are rehypnotized. Awaken the patient and then immediately rehypnotize them.

During reinduction, suggest or feed back to the patients their thoughts, feelings or sensations they experienced during their previous hypnotic state. Suggest that the patient will go even deeper as they experience these thoughts or sensations. This technique may be repeated several times until positive results of hypnotic analgesia can be demonstrated.

Dr. Longacre's Hypnodepthmeter

Dr. Longacre's Hypnodepthmeter technique allows the therapist to monitor the patient's subjective experience of the deepening procedure.

To use the hypnodepthmeter as a deepening technique, the therapist asks the patient to imagine a yardstick leaning against a wall with large easy to read numbers. The number thirty six is at the top of the yardstick and the number one is at the bottom.

The patient is then asked to picture and imagine a large white arrow that is next to the yardstick that can point to any number on the yardstick. Suggest that the arrow can move up and down the yardstick and that the numbers have special meaning. If the arrow points to the numbers 36 down to 25 it means the patient is in a light state of hypnosis. If the arrow points to the numbers 24 down to 13 it means they are in a medium state of hypnosis. If the arrow points to the numbers 12 down to 1 it means they are in a deep state of hypnosis.

The therapist has the patient picture and imagine the arrow moving down the yardstick and counts from ten down to one. The therapist should now ask the patient what number the arrow is pointing to. If the number is above 12, the therapist reassures the patient and then counts again from ten to one. When the patient imagines the arrow to be at the number 12 or less the therapist may begin the second step of the deepening procedure.

Suggest to the patient that the white arrow has been replaced with a red arrow that can move up and down the yardstick. The color red is easily recognized by the subconscious mind. Suggest to the patient that the numbers on the yardstick have a different meaning when the red arrow points to a number.

If the red arrow is pointing to the number 36 down to 25 it means they are in a very deep state of hypnosis. If the red arrow points to 24 down to 13 it means they are in a medium state of hypnotic anaesthesia and if the arrow points to the number 12 or less it means that they are in a deep state of hypnotic anaesthesia.

Suggest to the patient that the red arrow will move down the yardstick as you count from ten down to one. Repeat the counting procedure until the patient pictures and imagines the arrow pointing to the number 12 or less.

If a deeper state of hypnosis is desired, suggest that the arrow is now blue. The blue arrow changes the meaning of the numbers on the yardstick. If the blue arrow points to the numbers 36 down to 25 it means the patient is in a very deep state of hypnotic anaesthesia and feeling only minor discomfort or pressure. If the arrow is pointing to the numbers 24 down to 13 it means that they are in a marvelous and peaceful state of hypnotic anaesthesia and feeling only pressure. If the blue arrow points to the number 12 or less it means they are in a total and complete state of deep deep anaesthesia and will remain in this wonderful, peaceful and beautiful place until it is time for you to awaken them.

A word of caution. Often a patient will become so deeply relaxed during Dr. Longacre's Hypnodepthmeter deepening procedure that they will choose to ignore the therapist's voice. This may result in an unpleasant experience for the therapist. No harm will befall the patient if they choose to ignore awakening suggestions. The patient will enjoy hypnotic sleep and then enter into a period of natural or physiological sleep and awaken naturally when they desire to do so. However, this can be a most perplexing experience for the therapist.

When using Dr. Longacre's Hypnodepthmeter deepening technique, the therapist should give the following suggestion while the patient is in a light or medium state of hypnosis.

"If you choose to ignore my voice or become so relaxed and comfortable that you no longer hear my voice, you will be able to hear and respond to my suggestions when I touch your shoulder and you are hearing my voice."

Hypnotic Anaesthesia Techniques

Dissociation can provide analgesia by allowing the patient to separate a body part from their consciousness. The body is a robot theory offers a good explanation of how dissociation works in therapeutic hypnosis. The dissociation technique suggests to the patient that a certain body part is perceived by the subconscious mind to be in another place or position than the body part is thought to be by the conscious mind.

The following case study is a good example of the dissociation technique.

Paula C., a nine year-old-girl, was admitted to the surgical intensive care unit of a major teaching hospital. She had earlier presented in the emergency room with head trauma due to an auto versus pedestrian accident. Surgery to control intracranial bleeding had been performed.

Upon admission to the SICU, Paula was responsive and alert but in a mild state of respiratory distress. Oxygen therapy was ordered via nasal canula at 3 liters per minute.

Auscultation revealed bilateral breath sounds with scattered rales and equal ventilation. Her breathing pattern was shallow and regular. Due to her neural status, arterial blood gas analysis was ordered for every half hour to monitor the oxygenation and ventilation status of the patient.

The drawing of an arterial blood gas sample is an uncomfortable procedure. If the patient is tense and anxious or the respiratory therapist has difficulty in locating a selected artery, the procedure can be most unpleasant if not painful.

Due to the frequent drawing of ABG samples and tiny arteries that were difficult to locate, this delightful child was soon in a state of fright every time a white uniform approached her bed. The nurse who was in charge of the patient also found it difficult to comfort this little girl when a blood sample had to be drawn.

The nurse requested that I hypnotize the patient and induce hypnotic analgesia before the next blood gas sample was drawn. Due to the patient's neural status, chemical analgesia was contra-indicated.

Hypnosis was rapidly induced by having the little girl concentrate on a teddy bear lapel pin that I held in my hand. I instructed her to watch the teddy bear without moving her head. After moving the teddy bear to a position above the top of her head, I suggested that her eyelids would soon become sleepy. When I observed her eyelids fluttering, I suggested they were becoming sleepy and very heavy and that it was alright to let them close and go deep asleep. I further suggested that as the eyelids went even deeper asleep, she would be able to see a television screen.

Imagery was then suggested that allowed her to turn on the television and see a picture of a colorful stuffed animal she was holding in this special magic television set. I suggested that she would see the animal more clearly as her body went deeper asleep and described the colors and features of the stuffed animal.

When clinical signs of hypnosis were observed I suggested that she imagine her right arm to be comfortably folded in her lap. I explained that I was going to lift the arm and as I did, the arm would start to tingle and then go deeply asleep like her eyelids and be numb. I further explained that when I let go of the arm it would float back to her lap. I then positioned the arm alongside her body to facilitate the drawing of a blood gas sample.

I asked her to nod her head when she saw her arm folded across her lap. When she gave a positive response, I instructed the nurse to draw the required sample.

The nurse then proceeded to draw the sample from the little girl who appeared to be sleeping. When the needle penetrated the skin, the patient gave no indication of physical discomfort or pain.

The first attempt to draw a sample from the patient's right arm was unsuccessful. The nurse remarked that she would have to try again using the little girl's other arm. The nurse was astonished when the youngster extended the other arm without opening her eyes. Again the patient did not appear to feel any pain or discomfort and the sample was successfully obtained.

I suggested to the patient that I would count from one to three and on the number three she would awake. I suggested that after awakening, she would not feel an "owie" and both of her arms would feel normal and nice.

Upon awakening, this charming little girl did not express any experience of discomfort in either arm. She was subsequently able to deeply relax whenever a nurse or therapist came near her bed.

Dissociation technique suggestions illustrated in this case study were having the little girl imagine that her arm was no longer a part of her body and in a different position than her conscious mind perceived it to be. Since the body cannot think and the subconscious mind perceived that the arm was no longer a part of her body or subject to the feeling of pain, hypnotic analgesia occurred.

Disorientation technique suggestions can guide the patient to another place and time. When the patient leaves a place or time of anticipated pain or discomfort, the subconscious mind can perceive pain stimuli as being only pressure. Disorientation is the technique of choice for elevating a patient's pain threshold.

Suggestions for disorientation should direct the patient to picture and imagine a calendar showing the present month, days of the month and the numbers for each day. The patient is then asked to imagine that the components of the calendar are disappearing. First the numbers on the calendar, then the days and finally the name of the month are suggested to disappear. When the calendar page is blank, suggest to the patient that they are now in another place and time and protected from harm or discomfort.

The therapist may also suggest to the patient that they are picturing and imagining a large bold face clock with easy to read numbers. The patient is then instructed to imagine all the numbers on the clock disappearing. When the clock face is blank, suggest to the patient that they are in another place and time and free of any discomfort or unpleasant sensations.

Safe place imagery may also facilitate disorientation and hypnotic analgesia.

Safe Place Imagery Script

After the patient has been placed in a state of hypnosis, suggest a standard deepening procedure and then continue with the following script.

And now drifting down, deeper and even deeper relaxed . . . And if you will . . . if you really wish to become even more deeply and completely relaxed and comfortable . . . Just allow yourself to be transported across time, across space . . . to a place . . . that to you means peace . . . comfort . . . safety and happiness . . . This is the first place in your awareness that means those things to you . . .

Begin to experience if you will . . . all the sensations of peace . . . comfort . . . safety . . . and . . . happiness . . . This is the first place that you have in your awareness that means those things to you . . . Now let yourself . . . allow yourself to experience all the sensations of peace, comfort and happiness. And you are beginning to look at all the things there are to see . . . And listen to all the sounds there are to hear . . . And smell all the aromas . . . And taste and touch whatever you wish to taste and touch . . .

And recognizing and realizing that as you experience all the parts of this place . . . The feelings of peace, comfort, safety and happiness . . . are being taken deep within you . . . And being moved around to all the parts of you . . . So that all parts of you know these feelings as you go deeper and even deeper relaxed . . . So comfortable, so peaceful and so content . . . so very very relaxed and calm . . .

And each moment you spend experiencing this safe place . . . The feelings become stronger . . . and more a part of you . . . You are enjoying this safe place more and more . . . And enjoying this safe place and your enjoyment is heightened every moment you spend there . . . So for a few moments just enjoy that very special safe place . . . And experience and ultimately know all the parts of this safe place . . . And enjoy the feelings interacting with you.

In this safe place you're feeling and experiencing all emotions in their proper perspective . . . And you are recognizing and realizing that you can keep all of these wonderful feelings with you in your normal waking state . . . And you can feel all the emotions clearly and completely and enjoy the benefits of this skill that makes you feel good.

You can return to this safe place any time you desire to do so. See yourself in this safe place now . . . Feel yourself in this safe place now . . . Enjoy this marvelous and wonderful safe place now and relax even deeper . . . and deeper. So very relaxed and so very safe now . . . And relaxing more and more in this very special safe place.

I am going to awaken you in a few moments . . . but when I do you will be able to return to this safe place whenever you desire to do so . . .

To return to this wonderful . . . marvelous . . . relaxing and safe place . . . all you have to do is close your eyes and take a few deep relaxing breaths . . . And as you breathe deeply you will be able to picture and imagine this wonderful safe place . . . And you are enjoying this safe place . . . and all the things that make this place so special to you.

And when you are in this safe place all the parts of your body are deeply . . . completely and totally relaxed . . . And all the parts of your body that are feeling tension just seem to relax . . . And relaxing even more and feeling only pressure in those parts of your body.

Go to this very special safe place now . . . Enjoy this wonderful place . . . And waiting for me to awaken you . . . Allow yourself to enjoy this marvelous safe place . . . until I awaken you . . .

Glove anaesthesia is a hypnotic technique that allows the patient to anaesthetize a portion of their body by touching that portion with their hand. A patient can usually be taught the glove anaesthesia technique in two to three therapy sessions.

To teach a patient how to employ glove anaesthesia; induce hypnosis, perform a standard deepening procedure and then give them the following suggestions: "I want you to concentrate on your right hand now. And as you go deeper and even deeper, concentrating on the right hand, you are finding that the hand is beginning to tingle, and becoming slightly warm or slightly cool, and beginning to feel numb."

"I am going to stroke the top of your hand and count from three down to one. And as I count the hand will become numb. Each number will make the hand more numb and feeling like a wooden board or a piece of driftwood. And on the numeral one the hand will be completely and totally numb and feeling only pressure. And the hand is becoming numb as I count three, very numb now, two . . . and completely numb, totally numb, one."

At this point the therapist should test the patient to determine that a feeling of numbness or hypnotic anaesthesia exists in right hand. The following pinch test must be used with caution to avoid an unpleasant experience for both the therapist and the patient.

Before beginning the pinch test, ask the patient to nod their head if their hand is now completely and totally numb. If they do not nod their head, repeat the above suggestions. Perform the pinch test only when the patient has indicated that they are experiencing a feeling of numbness in their hand. The following suggestions are used for the pinch test:

"I am going to touch the top of the right hand now and you will feel only pressure. The right hand feeling only pressure." Pinch the top of the hand between your fingernails.

"Now I am going to pinch the top of your left hand. Just a tiny pinch so you will know I have gently pinched the top of your other hand." Now lightly touch the top of the left hand. "When I awaken you, you are remembering the hand that I pinched."

Awaken the patient and ask them to show you which hand you pinched. They will generally indicate the hand you touched. Show them the marks your fingernails left in the top of the hand you said you touched but did in fact pinch.

By having the patient observe the pinch marks, the therapist can demonstrate to the patient that they were in a state of hypnotic anaesthesia and reinforce expectation of positive results and belief in other glove anaesthesia suggestions.

Conclude the first glove anaesthesia training session by rehypnotizing the patient and then suggesting that the feeling of numbness in the right hand can be transferred to another part of their body.

Formulate therapeutic suggestions that enable the patient to transfer the feeling of numbness from their hand to a side of their face. Ask them to nod their head when the side of the face is numb. Suggest that the side of the face that is numb will remain this way after they awaken, until you tell them their face is normal again. Now alert the patient and ask them to pinch both sides of their face. They usually report a feeling of numbness on the side of the face they touched with their hand. Be sure to remove the above post hypnotic suggestion before terminating the therapy session.

In future training sessions, formulate glove anaesthesia suggestions that enable the patient to experience this phenomena in other parts of their body. The therapist should also reinforce their ability to rapidly induce self-hypnosis and employ the glove anaesthesia technique.

The protective shield technique is another type of imagery that can be used for hypnotic anaesthesia. The protective shield technique is discussed in the chapter on Pain Management.

CHAPTER 11

Hypnodontics

Aaron Moss, D.D.S., coined the term "Hypnodontics" to dispel the myths about hypnosis for dental patients who could be helped with this safe, effective and natural health care alternative to chemical analgesia. Hypnosis in dentistry had been proven to be effective in alleviating unpleasant experiences associated with dentistry. Though many myths about hypnosis still prevail, the efficacy of hypnosis in dentistry has been well documented in modern medical literature.

Indications

Selected patients can experience painless dentistry by using self-hypnosis. A local anaesthetic can provide analgesia for a majority of dental patients but the effects of local analgesia may be less than desirable due to the patient's anxiety, tension or fear of the dental procedures.

Indications for hypnodontics or hypnotic anaesthesia for dentistry include the following:

1. Elimination of the patient's tension, anxiety or fear of pain and related discomfort.

2. Accustoming the patient to orthodontic or prosthetic appliances after the patient has agreed to accept them.

3. Maintenance of the patient's comfort during long and arduous periods of dental work.

4. Modification of noxious dental habits like bruxism, unconscious grinding of the teeth.

5. Reduction of anaesthesia or analgesia during dental procedures.

6.   Substitution for, or in combination with, premedication for general anaesthesia.

7.   Amnesia for unpleasant work.

8.   Prevention of gagging and nausea.

9.   Control of salivary flow.

10.   Control of bleeding.

11.   Postoperative analgesia.

Precautions

The major precaution for the use of hypnosis in dentistry is symptomatic pain removal. Professional hypnotherapists should not attempt to deal with symptomatic pain due to oral dysfunction or disease without consulting with a dental physician.

Allied dental professionals should attend a state approved training program before assisting the dentist with hypnotic induction or hypnodontic therapy.

Clinical Applications

Modern dental techniques and preventative care has enabled a majority of patients to experience a relatively painless and unremarkable dental appointment. However, this is not the case for 'fussy' patients.

Fussy patients often put off going to the dentist until the pain or dental problem can no longer be ignored. These patients, for a variety of reasons, are fearful, tense, nervous and anxious before and during the dental visit. Often these fussy patients will request a tranquilizer or complain of extreme anxiety one or two days prior to seeing the dentist for a simple check up.

Fussy patients may be a small minority in the population of an average dental practice however, they often present the majority of problems the dentist encounters in his daily routine. Fussy patients take extra time and require special consideration by the dentist and his staff.

Hypnosis can readily ameliorate the tension, nervousness and unreasonable fear of pain often exhibited by fussy patients. The hypnotherapist should meet with this type of dental patient two or three days prior to the scheduled dental appointment.

After inducing hypnosis, have the patient imagine their special or favorite place. This should be a place that always makes them feel safe, happy and relaxed. Ask the patient to recall all of the feelings, sensations and memories about this place using their five senses. Suggest two or three word pictures of different places like the mountains, the seashore or a country lane or meadow.

When painting this word picture you might say something like, "So that if you are in the mountains you are smelling the aroma of the pines, feeling the sun gently warming your face, picturing the clean blue sky and marveling at the shapes of soft white puffy clouds lazily floating by," etc. It is not necessary to solicit information from the patient regarding the place they are recalling or remembering.

Before awakening the patient give them a post-hypnotic suggestion that they will be able to relax as deeply as they are now and enjoy this special place as soon as they sit down in the dental chair or lounge. Instruct them to close their eyes when they sit down in the dental chair and take three deep breaths. Suggest that every time they do this they will instantly relax and enjoy their favorite place.

Other applications of hypnosis in dentistry include; hypnotic anaesthesia, adaptation to oral control of bleeding, salivation, the gag reflex and post-operative analgesia.

To help a patient adapt to a dental prosthetic device, induce hypnosis and then give strong and positive end result imagery suggestions. These suggestions should reinforce how comfortable the patient is with the appliance, how nice they look and how confident they feel when wearing the appliance. Post-hypnotic suggestions should be directed at how comfortable the appliance will be in the wake state.

Suggestions for the control of bleeding, salivation and gagging should paint word pictures of tissue healing and blood vessels becoming smaller. Suggest that the mouth is very dry during periods of dental work and the gag reflex is inoperative until the patient is awakened or alerted by the dentist.

Suggestions for post-operative analgesia should reinforce the desired outcome or goal of the dental procedure. Post-hypnotic suggestions should be directed at having the patient picture and imagine the tissue in their mouth healing quickly, nicely and normally and as the tissue heals they are experiencing only pressure and a relaxing sensation of numbness.

Needless to say, if a post-operative problem that is not a part of the normal and natural healing process manifests, these suggestions will be rejected by the patient. Suggestions for postoperative analgesia should always emphasize normal and natural healing to prevent possible complications due to the patient delaying to ask for professional dental or medical advise.

CHAPTER 12

Pain Management

Much of the pain we experience in our daily living is due in part to stress and tension. Hypnosis has been proven to be effective in the alleviation of stress and tension. The subjective experience of pain is also related to a variety of psychogenic factors such as the fear of pain and the conditions and circumstances surrounding the "pain experience."

Hypnosis is indicated for the management of psychogenic pain and is also useful for the management of physiological pain resulting from acute trauma or disease.

There are two general classifications of pain, acute and chronic. Acute pain is associated with a sudden onset and is generally more intense than chronic pain. Chronic pain is usually of an ongoing nature and the intensity may vary.

Since pain can be a warning signal of physiological dysfunction as well as the result of tension or stress, a differential diagnosis must be made as to the origin of the pain. Before beginning hypnotherapy for pain management, the hypnotherapist should refer the patient to a physician for professional medical advice. The therapist should also ask the patient to provide a medical referral or prescription for pain management therapy.

If the therapist fails to obtain a medical referral, they may be responsible for the exacerbation of the patient's condition. For example, acute low back pain may be an indication of muscular strain. Acute back pain may also be an indication of a herniated or ruptured disc. If the patient's back pain is due to a problem with a disc, hypnosis is not only contraindicated but may mask symptoms and predispose irreversible nerve damage.

Hypnotherapy for acute pain is beneficial for many burn and trauma patients but should only be given under the supervision of a medical doctor. The most frequent indications for hypnotherapy for pain management centers around physiological and psychogenic chronic pain.

Before formulating a treatment plan, the hypnotherapist should have a basic understanding of the psychology of pain.

The Psychology Of Pain

There are many types of pain. From the time of birth we give the word pain a different meaning. Infants feel the pain of hunger. Adolescents feel the pain of conflicting emotions and adults feel the pain of physical exertion. We learn from the time of birth how to cope with pain. When our painful experience is associated with a traumatic injury or event, we learn the fear of pain.

The subjective experience of pain is a combination of the type of pain we are experiencing and our fear of that pain. Often the fear of pain intensifies as we grow older and become aware of our helplessness to control physical or traumatic pain.

When we experience traumatic pain, we become aware of our mortality which often increases our fear of pain. This fear of pain often exacerbates a variety of chronic conditions and the severity of pain associated with these conditions.

Pain can be a warning signal of physiological dysfunction but it can also be a way to cope with an emotional problem. Many people find that their pain is a tool that can be used to manipulate others. Often these people do not benefit from pain management therapy because they need their pain.

A detailed explanation of the psychology of pain is beyond the scope of this text, however, there are several important questions that the therapist should ask before formulating a therapy plan. The patient should be questioned about the onset of their problem, i.e., the date, circumstances surrounding the onset such as trauma or injury and their fear of the painful experience. It is also helpful to know the patient's previous efforts to alleviate the problem and the results of these efforts. Other questions should be directed at finding out how the patient's problem has changed their life, what is the patient's present quality of life and does the patient need the pain.

If the patient truly desires to ameliorate or manage their subjective experience of pain, hypnotherapy and guided imagery can benefit a majority of pain management cases.

Pain Management Therapy

Pain causes tension and a tightening up of affected areas in the body. Our normal response to pain is to resist the pain by tightening up even more and becoming more tense. This exacerbates the severity of the pain experience. Hypnotherapy can help patients learn how to relax the affected areas of the body causing pain and ameliorate concomitant fear, stress and tension.

Psychogenic pain may be alleviated with imagery that enables the patient to dissolve and dismiss the pain. An example of this type of imagery is presented in the Pain or Anxiety as the Object Script. Physiological pain can be put away outside the body as suggested in the Protective Shield Script.

Glove anaesthesia and safe place imagery are also effective for pain management therapy.

Pain management therapy is enhanced when the patient is taught self-hypnosis and is able to reinforce therapeutic suggestions at home or work. There are many methods for teaching a patient self-hypnosis. The method presented in this chapter is a combination of several different methods and has been proven to be an easy to understand and effective technique.

While the patient is in a hypnotic state, suggest that they concentrate on their right hand. As they concentrate on their right hand, suggest that the hand is becoming slightly warm or cool. Ask them to nod their head when the right hand is slightly warm or cool. If a positive response is not given, suggest that they go deeper relaxed and repeat the suggestions.

When the patient indicates that the hand is slightly warm or cool, suggest that they will experience this feeling when practicing self-hypnosis. This suggestion should be repeated as a post hypnotic suggestion.

Now suggest to the patient that they will be able to return to this comfortable feeling of hypnosis any time they desire to do so by using the eye elevation, focal point technique described in the chapter on hypnotic childbirth.

After alerting the patient, talk them through a self-induction and suggest that they are experiencing all the pleasant sensations of deep relaxation and hypnosis. Suggest that the patient picture and imagine a clock with large easy to read numbers and can see or hear the minutes ticking by. Suggest that they continue to deeply relax until three minutes pass by and that they will then open their eyes and feel alert and normal in every way.

When the patient is able to demonstrate a satisfactory level of self-hypnosis, the therapist may proceed to instruct the patient in the use of auto suggestion techniques. These techniques may include picturing and imagining the safe place they experienced during the therapy session or pain or anxiety as the object imagery. The protective shield image may also be used with self-hypnosis.

The patient may wish to formulate their own auto suggestions. A simple way for them to do this is to write down a short statement that is beneficial for them. Examples are; the pain in my back is leaving my body, I am feeling better and better in every way and I am enjoying my favorite place.

Instruct the patient to write their statement on a file card or piece of paper in large easy to read letters. Tell them to open their eyes and scan the statement after they have induced self-hypnosis. caution the patient not to try to read the material, simply look at it for a few seconds and then close their eyes.

Now the patient should set their imaginary clock to alert them in two to five minutes.

The patient should be encouraged to practice self-hypnosis and auto suggestion daily until their next therapy session. A progressive relaxation induction tape with therapeutic suggestions may be given to patients who are experiencing difficulty with self-induction.

Teaching the patient an effective way to induce self-hypnosis is one of the most important elements of pain management therapy.

Pain Or Anxiety As The Object Imagery

And relaxing deeper and deeper . . . drifting way down now . . . Deeper and even deeper relaxed . . .

And recognizing and realizing how many of us experience sensations that we would regard as unpleasant . . . Tension, discomfort, stress and strain . . . And we have already learned one method of dealing with these . . . and that is . . . just breathing deeply and removing all parts of stress and strain . . .

And using another image now . . . another image that can bring us peace, comfort, contentment and deep relaxation . . . Another method that is so powerful, it can remove all the symptoms of stress and strain . . . The symptoms of stress and strain are all very subjective feelings . . . We feel them, but as we know only too well it is difficult to consciously modify our feelings . . . and it is much easier to modify objects . . . And so we are now changing our unpleasant sensations into objects.

If you are experiencing pain or discomfort . . . or if you feel somewhat tense or anxious . . . I want you to take that unwanted feeling, tension, stress or tight muscle . . . and give it a shape . . . Just imagine that shape. Allow yourself to visualize that shape . . . It can be an abstract shape or a concrete shape.

And it can be an object . . . or a geometric design or it can be soft. It can be a color . . . Whatever shape first comes into your mind . . . is the right shape or object for you . . . Don't try to force the shape . . . just let it happen . . . as you go deeper and even deeper relaxed . . . And you are doing so very well . . . so peaceful, calm and relaxed.

And just relaxing . . . going deeper and even deeper. Give that shape a color . . . Just imagine the size of the shape And you can give it a size just by knowing its size . . . or just by picturing it next to an object you know the size of. And you are recognizing and realizing that the shape is a symbol of your tension . . . stress . . . strain . . . anxiety or discomfort . . . And the larger the shape is the more severe the discomfort is. And the smaller the shape is . . . the less the discomfort is . . .

And practicing now . . . first making the shape larger . . . and then making it smaller . . . And when you make the size of the shape bigger it is easier to make the shape . . . smaller . . .

If you have difficulty making the size of the shape smaller. Then use a few tricks . . . If the shape is a balloon you can put a needle into it . . . or kick it away . . . throw it away . . . Put it on a boat or a truck . . . or tie it to the tail of an airplane or bird . . . and let it fly away with it . . .

And realizing that as this symbol is becoming smaller . . . the feelings associated with it are becoming less intense . . . And you can make it smaller . . . As small and comfortable as you want to make it . . . And you are making it smaller by practicing making it larger and then smaller . . . And you realize that these are skills and as with any skill . . . The more you practice the more powerful the skill becomes . . .

And you can use this skill any time you desire . . . The more you practice the easier it is for you to allow these skills to be totally and completely effective . . . So very easy to use and so very powerful . . . anytime you choose to use this skill . . .

And you are practicing making the shape smaller and the color of the shape fade . . . And every time you do this it is easier and even easier . . .

I am going to let you rest for a moment but when I awaken you . . . you will find that you can give the shape a size and a color . . . and then instantly . . . effortlessly . . . easily . . . make the shape smaller and the color fade . . . And every time you do this it becomes easier and even easier . . . And when I awaken you the shape is fading and becoming smaller . . .

The Protective Shield Image

Just allow your body to rest now . . . And relaxing deeper and even deeper . . . Drifting way down deeper and even deeper . . . And as you go deeper and deeper . . . all distractions seem to disappear . . .

I want you to concentrate now on your breathing and feel all the tension leaving the chest area each time you exhale . . . Feel yourself . . . allow yourself to relax even deeper with each breath . . . And your breathing is becoming more regular . . . And with each breath you are breathing slower . . . And relaxing . . . breathing more regularly . . .

And your breathing is so easy now . . . so relaxing and comfortable and your entire body is relaxing more and more with each and every breath you take.

Feel your entire body completely and totally relaxing as you continue to drift even deeper down . . . Let yourself . . . allow yourself to feel and imagine this wonderful warm sense of relaxation and going even deeper relaxed now . . .

And you may have noticed that some areas of the body are more easy to relax . . . And concentrating on the areas of your body that you find to be the most comfortable . . . the most relaxed . . . And as you concentrate on these areas . . . you are recognizing and realizing what there is about those areas that makes you so comfortable and so very relaxed . . . And feeling all the sensations in those areas . . . the most relaxed and comfortable parts of your body . . .

And now you are allowing the comforting sensations of the most relaxed areas to spread . . . And as this marvelous sensation spreads to other parts of the body the feeling of relaxation becomes stronger and even stronger . . . And the relaxation spreads now out beyond those areas . . . And continues to spread to all the parts of the body you desire to relax deeper and even deeper.

Picture and imagine that this relaxation spreads like the rays of the sun . . . gently . . . warming and relaxing . . . or like rings of water spreading from a pebble tossed into a quiet pond . . . Picture and imagine this relaxation spreading to every cell in your body . . . And allowing yourself to enjoy this tranquil and peaceful relaxation in every nerve . . . fiber . . . bone . . . and cell in your body . . .

And with every passing moment . . . this feeling of deep, tranquil and comforting relaxation . . . becomes stronger in every part of your body . . . And every cell of your body knows and enjoys this wonderful sensation . . .

And this wonderful feeling now goes out beyond the physical confines of your body . . . Spreading out beyond the skin to form a protective shield around you . . . And you can let this feeling spread far. far beyond your physical body . . . or keep it close like a second skin . . .

And since this protective bubble or shield is your own creation you can do with it what you wish . . . You can use this shield in any way you want to . . . The uses of this shield are limitless . . . It can act as a filter . . . to filter out those feelings or things going on around you . . . And filtering situations that are uncomfortable . . . and allowing you to let in those feelings you wish to let in and experience . . . And it can act as an amplifier to help you understand people . . . and people to understand you . . .

And it can be invisible or visible to a few people or as many people as you want it to be . . . And you are using this protective shield any way you choose to use it . . . and that's O.K. because this shield is your own creation.

And you are using this shield and enjoying comfort in every part of your body . . . Practicing and using this shield . . . and allowing it to spread . . . And allowing it to go beyond the confines of your physical body . . . And you can experiment with it . . . Making it as large as you like . . . Using it as a transport to another place or time . . . And the more you use it the stronger it becomes . . .

In just a moment I am going to alert you to this time and place . . . But when I do you will be free of all tension and stress in your body . . . And recognizing that you can use this protective shield any time you desire to do so . . . And you are free of stress and tension . . . your body is completely and totally relaxed . . . rejuvenated and renewed . . .

———————————————

CHAPTER 13

Patient Education Materials

Patient education brochures and pamphlets are useful to enhance the patient's expectation of positive results with hypnotic childbirth, hypnodontics and pain management.

Educational brochures and pamphlets should dispel the myths surrounding hypnosis, explain how the patient can benefit from hypnotherapy and inform the patient as to what they can expect to happen when using a specific hypnotic anaesthesia modality.

In addition to enhancing patient expectation and understanding of hypnotic phenomena, educational materials enhance the therapist's prestige with individual patients and clients.

The therapist who elects to develop their own patient education brochures should make sure that their facts and statements are accurate and acceptable by the medical community as well as the patient. A poorly written brochure can do more harm than good. For information about obtaining preprinted brochures contact the National Board for Hypnotherapy and Hypnotic Anaesthesiology.

Patient education cassettes are useful to enhance patient expectation and reinforce therapy sessions.

The expectation of positive results from therapy is greatly enhanced when an expecting mother can listen to another patient's experience with hypnotic childbirth techniques. Hypnodontic and pain management patients can also benefit from listening to another patient's experience.

Recorded cassettes should present the same information for a specific type of therapy as given in patient education brochures and pamphlets.

Cassettes may also be recorded and used to reinforce the therapy session. These cassettes should include a progressive relaxation induction and imagery used during the session. Conclude the cassette by alerting the patient so that the cassette can be used at home between visits to the therapist.

Prerecorded cassettes for childbirth therapy and hypnodontics are available from the National Board for Hypnotherapy and Hypnotic Anaesthesiology.

The following patient education brochures are included to aid the therapist in developing their own educational materials. Therapists should not reproduce this material in any manner without the written permission of the author.

DEEP RELAXATION
AND
NATURAL CHILDBIRTH

A Joyful Family Experience!

Wouldn't it be great to have your baby without experiencing fear, anxiety or extreme pain. It is possible to have this kind of experience using a special process of deep relaxation, that can be incorporated with the childbirth method of your choice.

Anxiety, tension and fear are not natural body processes. They are the result of undue pressure and are often at the root of many diseases, allergies and chronic pain.

We need to learn how to alleviate our anxiety, tensions and fears especially during pregnancy and childbirth.

Tension in itself can be the cause of pain. An example is the common headache which is often caused by nervous tension. Nervous tension can also cause stomach ulcers, skin diseases and heart attacks. Tension can also complicate the natural process of childbirth.

Since the body accommodates every natural process, when it is functioning properly, pain can be a warning signal of malfunction or the result of tension, fear or panic.

In a natural process like childbirth there is a normal amount of discomfort, however, extreme pain is not a necessary part of the normal birthing experience. The discomfort of childbirth can be almost negligible when you are relaxed in both mind and body.

Labor is hard work . . . but it does not need to be painful. Hard work should leave you pleasantly tired and relaxed.

Briefly then, the pain of labor is due to tension caused by fear. This pain then intensifies the fear, which in turn increases the pain substantially. A vicious circle of three evils (tension, fear and pain) destroys confidence, relaxation and self control during labor.

With the aid of a professional trained in deep relaxation in childbirth, you can easily learn how to apply these techniques at work, at home, or in the hospital. Deep relaxation is highly indicated for both mother and child during pregnancy, labor and delivery.

Deep relaxation childbirth techniques can help you with the following experiences:

- Relief from morning sickness.

- Relief from low back pain and other discomforts due to body changes during pregnancy.

- Relief of headaches and other pain that can not be treated with medications due to pregnancy.

- Breathing techniques learned for labor and delivery can be easily remembered and performed without anxiety.

- Decrease the need of pain medication during labor and delivery.

- Your partner can participate in a joyful birthing experience free of worry, fear and anxiety.

- An immediate bonding with your baby.

Deep relaxation or hypnosis is like day dreaming. You feel relaxed, drowsy and comfortable but you are very aware of what is going on around you. You can ask and answer questions, follow instructions and hear your newborn baby's cry.

Relaxation is the goal of hypnotic childbirth. With relaxation comes a feeling of self-control, confidence, security, contentment and well being. Hypnosis can help you relax during childbirth more completely than any other method.

A professional trained in hypnotic childbirth acts as a guide to suggest and outline the course you wish to follow to attain relaxation of your body and mind.

You can awaken yourself from deep hypnotic relaxation at any time you desire to do so

YOU CAN
Relax during
Dentistry

Alleviate Fear
Alleviate Pain
Alleviate Tension

Help Your Child
have a better dental
experience

Dentists have always been concerned about their patient's comfort.

A dentist introduced anaesthesia in America after discovering the effects of nitrous oxide or laughing gas.

A group of dentists pioneered hypnodontics used today to help patients relax and have a better dental experience without fear, anxiety of extreme pain.

Anxiety, tension and fear are not natural body processes. We need to learn how to alleviate our anxieties, tensions and fears which are often at the root of many diseases, allergies and aggravated conditions.

- Anxiety, tension and fear can also cause pain.

- Tension in itself can be the cause of pain. The common headache usually is the result of nervous tension

- Nervous tension can cause stomach ulcers, heart attacks, skin problems and other distressing diseases.

- Tension can also intensify unnecessary discomfort during dental procedures.

There is a normal amount of unease associated with going to the dentist but this apprehension is almost negligible when you are relaxed both in mind and body.

Most unpleasant dental experiences are caused by tension due to fear. Anxiety then intensifies the fear which in turn increases tension and results in pain. A vicious circle of these three evils (tension, fear and pain) can destroy confidence, relaxation and self-control.

With the help of a professional, you can easily learn how to relax at home, work or at the dental office. Children can easily relax with this professional help.

Deep relaxation can help you experience the feeling of day-dreaming while in the dental chair. Though you feel relaxed, drowsy and comfortable, you are very aware of what is going on around you. You can ask and answer questions, follow instructions, hear your dentist's voice and most enjoyable of all, feel no pain.

Relaxation is the goal of hypno-dontics With relaxation comes a feeling of self-control, confidence, contentment, security and well being.

Hypnodontics can enable you to relax completely in a pain free dental experience.

Please be assured that nothing can be done during hypno-dontic relaxation that you do not approve of or that can cause you embarrassment.

You can awaken yourself from hypnodontic relaxation at any time you desire to do so.

Hypnodontics is a short cut to better physical and dental health for you and your family. Hypnodontics can help patients easily become accustomed to orthodontic or prosthetic appliances, modify noxious dental habits, prevent gagging and nausea and remain comfortable during periods of dental work. Less chemical anaesthesia is required with hypnodontics.

With hypnodontics, children learn that there is no reason to fear going to the dentist.

Please ask a member of our staff or your dentist about hypnodontics and how this can benefit you during your dental visit.

CHAPTER 14

Advanced Pain Management Techniques

A specialist in Hypnotic Anaesthesia for pain management is often requested to assist a client or patient in a medical setting by a physician who expects that a state of hypnotic analgesia or anaesthesia can be facilitated in six minutes or less. It is important that a specialist in pain management be able to understand and utilize the concepts of rapid inductions in medical settings that frown on theatrics or physical manipulation.

Rapid inductions (instant inductions) have often been demonstrated as part of a stage show conducted by a hypnotist. Because of the theatric nature of some of these induction techniques, the medical community has rejected this approach to inducing hypnotic anaesthesia and at the same time requested that a more efficacious rapid induction be available for their patients. The Hypno-Anaesthesia Therapist will want to develop their own rapid induction techniques based on the clinical concepts and application of suggestions that misdirect attention and bypass the analytical mind to help the patient enter a self-induced state of hypnosis. This approach to the rapid induction of hypnosis requires that the therapist be able to combine both verbal and non-verbal induction techniques in combination with creative imagery that is appropriate for a given client or patient.

While there are many different types of rapid inductions that rely on the "Jerk and Shout" method which utilizes suggestions and physical manipulation that results in momentary mental confusion or loss of equilibrium, these methods are generally contraindicated in a medical setting. However, it is important to understand the fundamental concept of why these inductions work and how to use this concept in a more medically acceptable manner.

How Rapid Inductions Work

There are two ways to help a client or patient enter a state of hypnosis. One way is to lullaby or bore the central nervous system with repetitive suggestions similar to a progressive relaxation technique. The other way is to provide suggestions that stimulate and excite the central nervous system and fire in a command such as "Sleep" which confuses the conscious or analytical mind and momentarily allows the subconscious mind to accept a suggestion of hypnotic relaxation. When the startling command "Sleep" is given, the patient is further distracted by feeling a forward or downward (non-verbal) motion that is the result of the therapist removing their hand from the client's hand.

The following series of suggestions are an example of a rapid induction that utilizes startling commands and non-verbal physical suggestions.

I want you to look at a spot on my forehead and concentrate on my voice. I am going to count from one to three. Put your hand on top of my hand and push down on my hand as hard as you can each time you hear the number. With each number, push down harder on my hand. Look right here on my forehead as I begin to count.

The client is seated in a chair and looking up to a spot on the hypnotist's forehead. As the hypnotist begins to count he moves the open fingers of his other hand up and down in front of the client's eyes.

I am going to count now and with each number you push harder on my hand and the eyes sleepy, tired, drowsy, the eyes so heavy and one, push down on my hand, and sleepy, tired, drowsy, push harder two, and sleepy, drowsy, the eyes so heavy and three, push hard.

As the client's eyes begin to close, the hypnotist rapidly pulls his hand out from under the client's hand, causing the client's hand to drop to their lap and at the same time says, "Sleep!"

The non-verbal forward and downward motion along with the startling command "Sleep" causes a momentary lapse of analytical or critical thinking and a brief state of hypnosis. In order to maintain a state of hypnosis the hypnotist must immediately begin suggestions that deepen the client's state of hypnosis.

———————

This type of rapid induction may be used with a client or patient that is in good physical health and presenting for an uncomfortable procedure in the dental office or a diagnostic area where profound relaxation is desired, however, it is contraindicated if the client or patient has suffered from any injury to the head or spinal column.

The concepts of this type of induction can be used with verbal and non-verbal rapid inductions that do not require physical manipulation. The principle elements that make this induction work are; Focused attention by the conscious mind, misdirection of attention by following simple suggestions and non-verbal suggestions of forward or downward movement. The concepts of this type of induction can also be reframed or restructured in a variety of Rapid Inductions that do not require physical manipulation or startling the nervous system with a loud command.

The following rapid induction imagery scripts illustrate how to combine the concepts of a high intensity induction with the relaxing scenario of traditional inductions which have been modified to take less than six minutes.

———————

Focal Point-Focal Point

Give yourself permission to feel comfortable in a matter of moments and look above your head as far back or above your head as you can and look for a magical spot that will soothe your body and mind and instantly provide a feeling of deep relaxation.

As you look for this spot notice how your eyes are already relaxing and looking for the spot so that they can close and relax your entire body. It is normal for the eyes to go down and close and every time they do, the whole body goes deeper down and relaxed, maybe the arms feel heavy or the chin seems heavy or the toes wiggle and just relax. And every time the eyes open or close the whole body relaxes and all the discomfort seems to fade.

If your eyes are closed, open them now and notice how heavy they are. Look at another spot above your head, don't move your head, just look at another spot on the wall or ceiling and tell the eyes to close. The eyelids are so heavy you do not need to open them. Make them heavy, sleepy, droopy and very relaxed. As long as the eyes are heavy and closed the whole body begins to feel more comfortable. You can enjoy this new feeling and sense of comfort just by keeping the eyes heavy, sleepy and closed.

Now test the eyes to be sure they are closed and go even deeper relaxed and every time you test the eyes you go deeper relaxed. Open the eyes and go deeper relaxed. Close the eyes and go deeper relaxed.

Now listening to my voice as you go even deeper relaxed and more comfortable until I ask you to awaken.

Helping Hands

Place your hands on top of mine. Push down a little on my hands. Feel my hands supporting yours as you push down and just close your eyes. Your eyes want to close and feeling my hands your body begins to relax.

And the question is, How does your body want to relax? Do you want to feel the warmth from my hands or a cool soothing feeling from my hands. Let yourself choose the relaxing feeling you want or just choose a feeling of helping hands that is best for you. Now make your hands heavy and then let them lift up a little. Now make your hands light as I push up on your hands. Let you hands stay light as I remove my hands. Now let your hands become heavy and relaxed and as they go deeper down to you lap, your whole body easily relaxes and you are concentrating on all the relaxation in your body. Notice the first part that starts to relax and then the next part and tell the whole body to go deeply relaxed.

Test this deep relaxation by stretching the fingers on your hand as you put them on top of your lap. Let the fingers stretch and relax just like you were yawning and wanting to sleep. And the whole body wants to relax and sleep as long as you picture and imagine that your hands are on your lap. Anyone can move your hands, however they are your hands and you picture and imagine that they are on your lap. Is that OK with you? Nod your head please.

Body Works

Make a fist with your right hand, now make a fist with your left hand, close the hand as tight as you can and then let the muscle go as relaxed as they can go. Now make the hand so relaxed that the toes of the feet tighten as hard as they can. Make the toes tighten and then relax. Notice how relaxed the hands are now and the toes become relaxed and may even stretch a little.

Now make your eyes tight, close the eyelids real tight and feel how relaxed the hands and toes are. Now let the eyelids relax and slowly open.

Put your hands on your forehead and let them slide down over your eyes and the hands tell the eyes to close and go even deeper relaxed. When the eyes close your chest relaxes and all the parts of your body relax so that you are breathing in pure relaxation and breathing out all the tension and all the muscles of the body relax more and more with every breath you take.

Imagine in your mind's eye the most relaxed place in your body and let that place relax the rest of your body. I am going to say the word "Sleep" three times. Each time you hear the word "Sleep" the body works better and goes even deeper relaxed. Each time you think sleep the head goes down, the body goes deeper down relaxing and all the tension leaves the neck and shoulders.

Bedside Thermometer

You are instantly entering a wonderful place of deep relaxation and comfort just by holding the bulb of the thermometer between your fingers. Look at the level of the mercury in the thermometer. Is the mercury red or blue or just a thin line? Look at the level of the thermometer and the question is, "Will the level go up with a pleasant warm feeling of comfort and relaxation or will it go down with a cool and soothing sense of relaxation?" Listen to my voice but watch the level of the thermometer.

Notice the numbers on the thermometer. What do the numbers mean? If the level goes up it means you are relaxing and if the level goes down it means you are relaxing. Now close your eyes and let the level go to the area of comfort that you desire. Give yourself permission to enjoy a deep sense of relaxation and no longer question why you are relaxing unless you wish to stop this sensation of increasing comfort and total relaxation of your mind and body.

Notice the relaxation you are feeling now and let this relaxation become a hundred times more powerful. Now double this relaxation again and take a deep relaxing breath and make the relaxation a thousand times more powerful until the whole body is feeling more relaxed than you have ever known yourself to be. Is that OK with you? Nod your head please.

Rapid Relaxation

Think about the top of your head or the bottom of your feet and the best way to relax them is to just close your eyes. And close your eyes and listen to my voice and all the parts of your body and mind that are relaxing instantly and rapidly. Listen closely to the first part that relaxes and then notice how easy it is to hear the next part. If the sounds are soft you are instantly relaxing. If you wish, let the sounds have another name or picture. See the sounds or just feel the sounds as the body instantly relaxes. Feel or imagine this relaxation rapidly going from the top of the head all the way down to the toes, or from the toes, spreading upward through the entire body to the top of the head.

With each and every breath the chest area relaxes and when the chest area is relaxing, nod your head please.

Please Note That The Above Imagery Scripts
Are To Be Used For Inductions Only

Appropriate Therapeutic Suggestions Should
Be Given After The Induction of Hypnosis

Using Suggestibility Tests as a Rapid Induction Technique

Suggestibility Tests are generally used to help the client or patient understand that they are able to use visualization and guided imagery techniques to accomplish the outcomes they desire. Hypnotists often use various tests to demonstrate how accomplished they are in inducing hypnosis. The well-trained hypnotherapist uses suggestibility tests to help the client or patient build a spiral of belief in his or her ability to successfully use imagery to create wanted change in their life.

The term "Test" implies something that you must do well to pass the class. The well trained hypnotherapist will recognize that

"Suggestibility Tests" are only a technique to persuade the client or patient to work with the therapist. No one wants to fail a test so they tend to cooperate with the therapist when taking a test. However, a well-trained therapist knows how to make any type of suggestibility test have a positive outcome.

Making The Dictionary and Balloon Test Work

If you are suggesting that one arm is heavy because there is a thick dictionary on the top of the hand and the other arm is light because a big bunch of helium balloons are tied to the wrist and one arm will go down while the other arm moves up and the client or patient does not react to these suggestions offered in the form of a test, the skillful therapist will make the test have a positive outcome by offering one of the following explanations.

"Of course your arm did not want to go up higher because you were so relaxed. It takes work to lift your arms and you were so relaxed that you did not want to lift one of your arms."

Of course your arm did not go down because you are always in control and accepting only suggestions that are helpful to you.

You didn't want to have a tired arm that was heavy, so you ignored this suggestion. Visualization and guided imagery works because you will only accept suggestions that are best for you."

The therapist can also make this test work by observing that despite suggestions that one hand is heavy and going down and the other hand is light and going up, the hands and arms do not seem to move. At this point, the therapist will want to offer the following alternative suggestions.

"And just relaxing even deeper, I am taking the dictionary off the top of your hand as you relax even deeper. Now turn the palm of your hand up and I am

placing the dictionary on the palm of your hand and
noticing the dictionary and the arm relaxes and goes deeper
down to the lap and the whole body relaxes."

When a client or patient responds well to a suggestibility test,
the therapist should realize that the test was a successful mini or
rapid induction. The following is an example of using a suggestibility
test as a rapid induction.

———————

Balloon and Dictionary

Your doctor has asked me to help you easily and
instantly become very comfortable and relaxed during your
procedure and I would like you to follow a few suggestions, is that OK with you?

Please close your eyes real tight for a couple of seconds
and then put your arms straight out in front of you. Now
keep your arms straight and even and let your eyes flutter
a little and the eyelids are light and closed. Test your eyes
to be sure they are light and closed. If the eyes are heavy let
them feel sleepy and listen to my voice. I will tell you
everything you will want to do. You do not have to open
your eyes and watch me. Tell your eyes to be comfortable
as you listen now. My voice will be soft and relaxing so
listen with your eyes closed.

Concentrate on your arms that are straight out in front
of you. On one hand I am placing a very heavy book or
dictionary and feel that arm supporting the weight of the
book. Notice your other arm as I tie a little string around
your wrist and use this little string to hold a big bunch of
balloons filled with helium, balloons like they use at parties
and these balloons will drift up higher and higher to the
ceiling as your arm begins to feel comfortable, relaxed and
so very light.

Now I am going to lift the heavy book from your hand and you let the hand feel heavy and you are relaxing the hand and the arm by letting it slowly drift down to your lap. I am going to let the balloons fly away now and your other hand and arm drift easily down to your lap. When the arms and hands are on your lap you are deeply relaxed and the whole body becomes so comfortable.

I am going to count out three numbers. As you listen to the numbers let your hands pretend to write each number or erase the number or just ignore the number as you go even deeper relaxed. Do what you want with the numbers or just ignore them and go even deeper relaxed.

One - Five - Three, and go way down, deep and relaxed as I count three numbers again. Seven - Two - One. Your eyes are so relaxed and heavy. As I lift an arm it feels so heavy and limp like a piece of cloth that seems to float away and the arms are heavy and fall down to the lap. The arms are so safe and comfortable in the lap. And as long as the eyes are closed the arms are safe in the lap, is that OK with you? Nod your head please.

If the head nod seems very relaxed, this is an indication that the client or patient has entered an acceptable state of hypnosis for an uncomfortable medical procedure. The therapist will notice that the more difficult it is to observe the client's or patient's ideomotor response of nodding the head, it is an indication of the depth of hypnosis achieved as a result of this rapid induction.

Creative Inductions

Many therapists rely on induction techniques that were developed by their instructors or other educators without realizing that the concepts of a rapid induction can be applied in the clinical setting utilizing the expressed desires and expectation of the client or patient. This concept is outlined in the book *Client-Centered*

Hypnotherapy." Creative inductions are developed by the therapist to fit a given time and situation presented by the client or patient. Creative induction requires that the therapist be comfortable with applying the concepts of the hypnotic formula in language that can be developed spontaneously to fit a wide variety of therapeutic outcomes.

The hypnotic formula (H = E + I + B + C) postulates that what you expect to happen, will happen, when you use your imagination. In other words, what you expect to happen, will happen if you believe it will happen. It is interesting to notice that this formula also works when the client or patient does not know what to expect to happen and comes to believe that something happened only because they allowed their imagination and their subconscious mind to find their own solution to the formula. An unexpected loud noise or sound may produce images of fear or anxiety the same way as the sound of gentle rain produces an unexpected feeling or sense of peace and relaxation. Seeing a picture or a scene in a movie that was not expected can also produce a negative or positive feeling in the mind's eye that is momentarily acted upon by the subconscious mind. When the subconscious mind has an opportunity to accept a visual, verbal or non-verbal suggestion in any form or manner of presentation, it can create a natural solution that is in the best interest of the client or patient.

The creative induction can be a simple story or metaphor or an unexpected series of suggestions that confuses or misdirects the left brain (conscious mind) and allows the right brain (subconscious mind) to create a new picture or image to enhance wellness, relaxation and restorative processes which are a natural part of the mind-body connection.

A good example of how a creative induction works was provided by a colleague who shared the story about a "Green Apple."

The pre-teen youngster was in the emergency room and the physician was putting stitches into his arm to close a rather large cut. The area had been numbed by a local anesthetic and the youngster should not have been feeling any pain. Despite the best efforts of the physician and the nurse, he kept screaming and carrying on so much that the physician was finding it difficult to close the wound.

A specialist in Hypnotic Anaesthesia came into the emergency room and was requested to do something quickly to comfort the boy so that the physician could finish closing the wound without using physical restraints on the youngster.

The Hypnotic Anaesthesiologist boldly pulled back the curtain to the Emergency Room cubicle, walked to the head of the treatment table and look at the youngster with a fixed stare. As soon as the youngster stared back at him he said, "Green Apples" in a loud and startling voice. The youngster stared back apparently speechless. The therapist continued to stare into the youngster's eyes. In the next five minutes the stitches were in and the procedure was over. The youngster never moved or flinched after hearing the command "Green Apples."

This is an example of an unexpected event, someone looking into the youngster's eyes and saying Green Apples that temporarily confused the conscious mind allowing the subconscious mind to search for a creative solution to the problem of anxiety, fear or discomfort. Because no further suggestions were presented to the subconscious mind, it had no choice but to ignore what was really happening as might be interpreted by the conscious or analytical mind.

Creative Induction Imagery Scripts

The following imagery scripts may be used to facilitate a rapid induction. These scripts are presented as an example of creative induction imagery and should not be read verbatim to a client or patient.

Crumpled Paper

"Take this piece of paper and crumble it up with your hands and make it into a shape or ball and then just look at it for a moment. Ask yourself if this paper can be a pretend object or toy or something else that reminds you of happy thoughts and relaxing feelings. Now hold the crumpled paper in the palm of one hand and gently close your eyes as you close your hand around the paper.

Now take a moment to concentrate on that crumpled piece of paper. Give it a name or color if that is appropriate for you. Feel the paper in your hand and make it smaller if you like or let it become soft and fluffy or change into something else.

As you go deeper relaxed the paper will be anything you want it to be and changing it into something that is relaxing for you, nod your head please. If you wish, you may pretend that the paper is like a soft fluffy cloud and you are floating on it or maybe watching the paper drift slowly by like a cloud in the sky. And your eyes are so relaxed and closed and the body is relaxed as you concentrate on the paper and all the other sounds and distractions around you seem to fade as you concentrate on the relaxing thoughts and feelings associated with the design you have created and are holding in your hand."

Appropriate therapeutic imagery would now be presented.

Slippery Pen

"I want you to hold this pen gently between your thumb and first finger. Hold the pen in the hand you normally write with. Look at the pen as you hold it and ignore everything else around you and look only at the pen. And the question is, why is this pen a special pen?

Concentrate on the pen and notice your breathing. Each breath gives the body clean, refreshing and life giving oxygen. When you breathe out notice how the chest area relaxes and how easy it is to gently hold the pen, but don't let it slip out of the fingers.

Now look at your other hand as you put the thumb and first finger of this hand together. Hold the thumb and first finger together as tight as you can. Now release the pressure between the fingers of this hand and the pen in the other hand seems to become slippery as if it was coated with oil or a slick covering. Don't watch the pen, concentrate on your other hand and watch the fingers of your other hand relax. They may want to come together for a moment and then open and the pen is so slippery it just seems to drop onto the table or floor and you go instantly deeper relaxed. Feeling the pen begin to slip or hearing the pen falling to the table or floor lets you go very deeply relaxed and there is no need to pick up the pen or worry about anything because your mind and body is so deeply relaxed. Is this OK with you, Nod your head please?"

After observing a head nod the therapist will continue with appropriate therapeutic suggestions.

Tighten And Relax

Put both your arms over your head and hook your hands together and pull on them hard. Feel the shoulders tighten as you pull on the hand, now let the shoulders relax and your arms go down to your lap.

Now tighten the toes on your feet as tight as you can. Pretend you are tightening your toes around a small object and tighten the toes as hard as you can. Now let the toes relax and stretch and become comfortable. Now I want you to close your eyes and picture and imagine your arms over your head and the arms and hands relax as they drift way down to your lap. Your eyes can feel sleepy now, is that OK with you? Nod your head please.

Now tighten your eyes and then let them relax and feel even more sleepy as your whole body goes deeper relaxed and the toes are relaxed and the hands relax.

Now I want you to tighten all the muscle and fingers of your hands as you hold them on your lap. Tighten real hard and then let the tension and anxiety go away as all the muscles and fingers relax again. All the muscles and fingers relaxing even deeper than before, and the whole body goes a hundred times deeper relaxed.

Now test the toes and notice how relaxed they are and nod your head please. Now test the hands and fingers and notice how relaxed they are and nod your head please. Now test the eyes and how relaxed the body is and nod your head please.

Tighten your shoulders one more time and then let them drop way down and the whole body goes even deeper relaxed.

Use a deepening technique and then continue with appropriate therapeutic imagery.

Inductions for People Who Object to Being Hypnotized

Most people who object to hypnosis do so because they have been misinformed about hypnosis. Visualization and guided imagery is a synonym for hypnosis. Imaging or Relaxation Therapy are also synonyms for hypnosis.

When working with pain management clients or patients, the therapist must be flexible when defining the natural God given process of using the mind to help and heal the body. Pain management therapists should emphasize that they do not hypnotize or control the patient in any manner. The pain management therapist is an instructor for self-help techniques that the patient wishes to learn.

When therapists who are recognized by the National Board for Hypnotherapy and Hypnotic Anaesthesioiogy as a Certified Hypno-Anaesthesia Therapist or a Registered Hypnotic Anaesthesiologist are asked about the type of therapy they provide, they answer, "I teach Visualization and Guided Imagery as a complementary medical modality for the alleviation or amelioration of unwanted or unnecessary fear, tension and anxiety concomitant with pain."

There are some people who object to the term hypnosis or hypnotherapy because they think their church objects to this type of therapy. These people can be helped with visualization and guided imagery that does emphasize the term "hypnosis."

In the book, *Client-Centered Hypnotherapy*, a chapter is devoted to helping people who object to hypnosis because of their religious affiliation. The main point of this chapter is that the concepts of visualization and guided imagery are the same concepts that therapists use when formulating ethical suggestions for hypnosis, relaxation imagery, prayer therapy and meditation.

When formulating suggestions to relax a patient or client, be aware that a complete explanation of what you are doing and why it will work is not needed. By spending a few moments actively listening to the client or patient can provide you with an induction method that will not be found in any book.

Active listening requires that the therapist listen, without interrupting, until the client or patient has completely expressed their thoughts. Information provided to the therapist should not be analyzed or have to match a behavior or thinking pattern accepted by the therapist.

It has been my experience that by just asking a patient to tell me what would help them feel more comfortable has provided the appropriate imagery for inducing hypnosis.

What would help you feel more comfortable?

SEEING MY GRANDCHILDREN

SITTING ON THE PORCH AT OUR BEACH HOUSE

AN EXTRA BLANKET ON THIS BED

A ROOM THAT ISN'T SO HOT

A TALL COOL DRINK OF WATER

SOMEONE I COULD TALK TO

FEELING THE KIDS HUG ME

BEING A CAREFREE YOUNGSTER AGAIN

SLEEPING IN MY OWN BED

HEARING MY DAUGHTER PLAY THE PIANO

BIG BAND MUSIC LIKE GLENN MILLER

Inductions were developed by simply providing end result imagery or suggestions that allowed the patient or client to picture and imagine that they were experiencing their request for comfort. The client or patient was asked to revivify a previous experience or picture and imagine that their request was now taking place as they closed their eyes and relaxed.

CHAPTER 15

Case Studies

————————————————————■————————————————————

Kathy S., Childbirth Patient

This intelligent and energetic young woman came to my office seeking counseling and advice about hypnotic natural childbirth. She was 29 years old and this was her first pregnancy. She appeared to be very anxious about the birthing process and fearful of the pain she had been told she would have to endure during her hospital experience.

During the clinical interview, this delightful lady explained that she had been fearful of doctors and hospitals since early childhood. Apparently she had injured herself while playing on a swing and was taken to a hospital for suturing of a cut next to her eye.

"I was frightened and afraid of everyone in the emergency room," said Kathy S. "The nurse asked my mother to leave and then I saw a big hand coming down to my face. The doctor said the needle wouldn't hurt, but it did. He kept poking the needle into my skin while I cried. I'll never forget how frightened I was, all alone and no one seemed to care."

As we talked, Kathy told me about other childhood experiences with doctors and hospitals. She had always had a problem with her weight and spoke of doctors who demanded she go on a strict diet or face a life of poor health.

Kathy appeared to be moderately overweight but stated that her health was generally good with the exception of a problem with high blood pressure. She was seeing an obstetrician for prenatal care and had registered for a prepared childbirth class.

Kathy told me that she was happily married and that her husband was very supportive and was trying to help her deal with her anxiety about childbirth. Despite the reassurance and support of her physician and husband, Kathy remained extremely nervous and fearful of her impending birthing experience.

I explained to Kathy how she could benefit by using hypnotic childbirth techniques and performed a standard series of suggestibility tests. Test results indicated that Kathy would be a good subject for hypnotherapy.

I devoted the majority of our first therapy session to alleviating her fears about childbirth. During the first session, she was able to achieve a very nice depth of hypnosis and left my office relaxed and expecting a joyful birth experience without unnecessary pain, anxiety or fear.

During our second childbirth session, Kathy indicated that she was having a problem with morning sickness. I determined that her problem was a psychogenic type of hyperemesis gravidarum and formulated appropriate suggestions which she readily accepted.

Kathy's physician asked that I help her learn to relax to reduce her blood pressure problem. I demonstrated a simple self-hypnosis relaxation technique to the patient. She was able to use this technique to overcome both her morning sickness and blood pressure problem.

Subsequent sessions were devoted to teaching Kathy how to use glove anaesthesia and hypnotic childbirth relaxation techniques.

Two days after giving birth to a healthy baby girl, Kathy called my office to tell me about her childbirth experience. The following is a transcript of our conversation.

Kathy: Dr. Longacre I had a baby girl, she is so pretty and so healthy, hypnosis really worked. I mean I didn't have a lot of pain and I was so relaxed all the time.

Dr. L: Congratulations, I know how happy you and your husband must be.

Kathy: My water broke but I didn't have any labor pains so I didn't know what to do. I called the hospital and a nurse said I should come in even if I wasn't in labor.

Dr. L: Were you using self-hypnosis to prevent feeling early labor?

Kathy: No, I was just relaxing I didn't think my baby was due for another two weeks.

Dr. L: When did you decide to go to the hospital ?

Kathy: I waited a couple of hours and then I started having contractions, so I called my husband at work. When he got home my contractions were still weak and irregular but we decided to go anyway since my water had broken several hours earlier.

Dr. L: How did you feel about going to the hospital ?

Kathy: Well, I was excited but I wasn't as nervous or anxious as I thought I would be. I really felt very confident about the whole thing. When I had a contraction, I just closed my eyes and took a few deep breaths. My husband was really calm too. I think that was because we went to a prepared childbirth class and because of our training in hypnosis for childbirth.

Dr. L: Tell me about your experience at the hospital.

Kathy: I had preregistered, so when we got to the hospital they took me right in to a labor room. I was on a monitor so they could check on the baby's heart rate and the strength of my contractions. When my contractions got stronger I decided to use self-hypnosis and make all the muscles work together I told myself that I was only feeling pressure. I was very calm and relaxed.

After two or three hours the doctor said he wanted to speed my labor up and the nurse gave me pitocin. Pitocin makes your contractions come close together and stronger.

Dr. L: Did the hypnotic childbirth techniques you learned help you after the nurse gave you pitocin?

Kathy: Oh yes, I was still feeling only pressure and was very relaxed. My contractions were very close together and a nurse said that they looked very strong on the monitor. Every time I felt a contraction starting, I used my hands to make my stomach feel numb. I did what we practiced together. I closed my eyes and counted from three down to one and let my whole body relax. I concentrated on my hands until they felt like they were numb. When my hands were numb I took three deep breaths and rubbed my stomach. All I felt with my contractions was pressure. I never felt any pain at all. I think the nurses thought I was an odd duck. They kept coming in and looking at the monitor and then at me. I remember one of them asking how I could be sleeping with contractions that were as close and strong as mine were.

Dr. L: Were you sleeping?

Kathy: (laughter) No. Of course not. I guess I looked like I was sleeping but I was just using self-hypnosis to relax deeper with each contraction. A couple of times I wanted to feel what labor was really like so I let myself have a labor pain. A couple of times was enough. I used my hypnosis during the rest of my labor and delivery. A few times I needed help from my husband. He squeezed my wrist and then I was fine and felt only pressure with my contractions.

Dr. L: Did the nurses help you use your hypnotic childbirth techniques?

Kathy: I don't think many of them realized what I was doing. My husband had given them the paper on hypnosis for childbirth but only one nurse said she had worked with a mother who was using self-hypnosis I remember one nurse who came in and asked lots of questions I don't think she believed me when I told her I was only feeling pressure. She wanted me to take some pain medication, I told her I didn't need it.

One nurse asked me if my labor pains were bad, my contractions really hurt then, until I started concentrating again on feeling only pressure.

Dr. L: Was it hard for you to concentrate on your hypnotic childbirth techniques in a busy hospital ?

Kathy: Sometimes it was. A lot of other women were whimpering and crying a lot. They were shouting obscenities and saying things like, "Oh God" and a lot of other words. I wanted them to be quiet. It was hard for me to relax with all that kind of noise going on around me. But when I wanted to ignore things that were upsetting me, my husband said, deeper and deeper and I could relax again.

Dr. L: How long were you in labor?

Kathy: Actually my labor went really fast. Since this was my first child, the nurses thought it would take a long time. I was in labor for about eight hours. In fact the nurses were amazed when they checked me and found that I was ready to go into the delivery room. I guess I fooled everybody. Even the midwife who delivered my daughter was amazed at how smooth things went for me. She said I didn't look like I had been in labor, not hard labor like you're supposed to have with pitocin.

Dr. L: Tell me about your delivery.

Kathy: When I was on the table in the delivery room, the midwife told me to push each time I had a contraction. I wasn't tired at all so I really pushed. I was pushing so hard, they had to tell me to stop pushing. I guess they weren't ready yet and I had almost pushed my baby out. The midwife told me to wait, so I used self-hypnosis to deeply relax until she said I should push again

The midwife wanted to give me a local anaesthetic to make my perineal area numb so she could make an incision so I wouldn't tear when my baby was born. I asked her to give me a minute to make the area numb myself.

She just looked at me. I think she thought I was going to do a magic trick. I told her the area was numb and I didn't need to have her deaden it and she could go ahead and make the incision. I didn't feel a thing.

I was so excited when I heard my baby cry. They put her on my stomach so I could hold her. She was so beautiful and she whispered little coos and cries. She seemed so content and peaceful.

Dr. L: Do you think your baby was so healthy because you didn't need an excessive amount of pain medication?

Kathy: Yes, I was glad I didn't need a lot of pain medication The midwife, nurses and the doctor were all amazed at how content my little girl was. She weighed seven and a half pounds and was twenty one inches long, but she looked so tiny.

They took my baby to the nursery to clean her up and have a pediatrician check her. By the time the midwife had finished sewing up my incision I had my daughter back in my arms. My husband and I went to a special family room with our daughter and took care of her by ourselves. We arrived at the hospital one morning and left the next. Everything was so perfect, just like you said it would be

Postscript

As we concluded our conversation, Kathy told me that she felt pleasantly tired after the birth of her daughter but enjoyed taking care of her at home without the discomforts she had been warned about. She said she was full of energy and her daughter seemed very content and slept soundly. Kathy used self-hypnosis techniques to take naps while her baby slept, and relieve the itching of stitches and other post-partum problems.

Kathy's daughter is now 12 months old. This infant girl smiles almost constantly and has never experienced colic or a fretful night.

Kathy attributes the techniques of hypnotic childbirth for her wonderful and joyful birthing experience and the glowing health and happiness she sees in her baby.

Kathy's experience is typical of the hundreds of mothers I have been privileged to work with.

Paul D., Hypnodontic Patient

A dentist who I work with asked me to come to his office and meet with Paul D. The dentist felt that hypnotherapy could help this patient overcome his anxiety and fear of dental work. Apparently this middle-aged man was extremely anxious about having two of his teeth crowned and had cancelled several appointments on the pretext that his job interfered with his dental appointments.

Paul's wife had read a brochure on hypnodontics while waiting to have her teeth cleaned and discussed the information presented in the brochure with her husband. Paul agreed that hypnodontics might be of benefit to him and asked his wife to make an appointment for him with the stipulation that hypnodontic therapy would be provided before he saw the dentist.

I met Paul at the dental office and found him to be very cooperative and interested in hypnosis.

During the clinical interview, Paul tried to convince me that he was not anxious or nervous about the dental procedure, but wanted me to hypnotize him so that he could feel what a hypnotic state felt like. He also informed me that he was trying to stop smoking. He stated that when he gave up cigarettes for a day he became nervous and craved fattening foods. Paul said he wanted to stop smoking but was afraid of becoming fat.

I proceeded to dispel the myths about hypnosis and explained how therapeutic hypnosis could benefit him during dentistry. Paul asked that I hypnotize him so that he could experience a painless dental visit.

I induced hypnosis with a progressive relaxation technique and proceeded slowly with this somewhat fearful patient. I presented suggestions that enabled the patient to picture and imagine that he was relaxing in his favorite place. A place that he could visualize, touch, smell and feel. A place that was calm and peaceful and always associated with pleasant memories. I then suggested that while he sat in the dental chair he would enjoy this very special place.

When Paul appeared to be in a light state of hypnosis I employed the yardstick deepening technique to deepen the trance.

Paul was able to see the yardstick and the numbers and easily went into a deep state of hypnosis.

I then suggested that he could totally enjoy this special place as soon as he sat down in the dental chair. I also suggested that when he closed his eyes and took three deep breaths he would sink a thousand times deeper and would experience only pressure in his mouth as the dentist completed the prescribed work

Therapeutic suggestions were then reinforced with post hypnotic suggestions. Before I alerted Paul, I also suggested that he would find that cigarettes would have a peculiar taste and this would remind him that he wanted to be a nonsmoker.

When the dental procedure was over, Paul stated that he felt like he had been day dreaming while in the dental chair. He reported that an hour in the dental chair seemed like just a few moments and he could not recall feeling any pain, only pressure. Paul said that when the dentist told him he would feel the pressure of a needle (used to inject a local anaesthetic), the needle felt soft and not unlike a toothbrush massaging the gums.

Paul thanked me for helping him experience a painless dental visit and was still talking about hypnosis for dentistry when he made an appointment for a follow-up visit before leaving the office.

Paul contacted me at my office two weeks later Paul seemed perplexed. He couldn't find a brand of cigarettes that didn't taste funny

He said he had tried every brand of cigarette available at his local market but they all tasted terrible and seemed to make him cough. He asked me to meet with him for non-smoking therapy because he didn't really want to smoke and cigarettes had lost the flavor he once had enjoyed. Paul did not recall the suggestion I had given him regarding cigarettes during his dental visit.

I encouraged Paul to come to my office and purposely neglected to mention my suggestion about cigarettes given during the dental visit.

Paul is now a non-smoker and is no longer anxious or nervous about going to the dentist. In his words, "I use self-hypnosis and just go fishing while I'm in the dental chair."

Sally M., Hypnodontics Patient

Sally M. was referred to my office by her dentist who had heard of my work with problem dental patients. Sally explained that she was having problems with her dentures and no matter how many times they were realigned, she still could not tolerate wearing them for more than an hour or two.

Sally's dentist informed me that he suspected that there was a psychological reason for her discomfort. He also stated that this elderly patient suffered from chronic gagging when putting in her dentures and during dental visits.

When I met this energetic 72-year-old lady at my office she was tearful and frustrated. She said she had tried everything and visited a number of dentists but nothing seemed to help her problem with wearing dentures. I carefully interviewed Sally regarding the circumstances surrounding the onset of her dental problem that resulted in her decision to wear dentures.

During the clinical interview we talked about how wearing dentures had affected her quality of life, her previous attempts to solve the problem and what she expected from hypnodontic therapy.

Sally explained that her problem had really started 40 years earlier.

"I had beautiful white teeth. I appeared in an advertisement for Colgate Toothpaste and was very proud of my smile. I developed a dental problem that caused the enamel on my teeth to chip. My dentist crowned several of my teeth but before they could all be fixed my husband died. I didn't have enough money to support my two children and still pay for all the dental work that had to be done."

Sally talked about the next couple of years and the hardships of being a widow. She told me how she met her second husband.

"My second husband is a wonderful and caring man. He accepted my children as if they were his own. We barely had enough money to make ends meet, but he worked hard to take care of us. He wanted me to have the rest of my teeth fixed, but I didn't feel it was right for me to ask him to bear the expense since he was already working so hard."

Sally said she was advised that she would have to have the rest of her teeth crowned or have them all extracted and dentures made. The cost of dentures was much less than having her teeth crowned. She explained that she decided to have her teeth pulled rather than ask her husband to pay for having her teeth crowned.

From the beginning Sally had gagged when putting in her false teeth and felt like she was no longer an attractive woman with a pretty smile.

Sally said she thought part of her problem was "in her head" and believed that hypnosis could help her. She was anxious about traveling back east to her daughter's wedding. She was worried about not being able to attend family functions because of her denture problem.

After inducing hypnosis, I suggested that Sally picture and imagine herself in front of her bathroom mirror and feel how comfortable her dentures were as she put them into her mouth. I emphasized how pretty she looked when she smiled and how normal and natural her dentures looked.

I further suggested that every time she experienced discomfort with her teeth, she need only take a few deep breaths, close her eyes and see herself in front of the mirror looking lovely. I suggested that when she did this, she would find that her gag reflex would go to sleep and her dentures would be attractive and comfortable.

Before alerting Sally, I gave her a post hypnotic suggestion that each time she put in her dentures, they would remain comfortable for a longer period of time and soon she would wear them all day long.

My second session with Sally was one week later on the morning of her scheduled dental appointment to have her dentures realigned. During our second session I reinforced the suggestions that her gag reflex would not bother her during the dental visit and she would find her dentures to be more and more comfortable with each passing day.

Post Script

Sally's dentist told me that he did not find anything wrong with her dentures and was amazed at the reversal of this patient's chronic gagging condition. Sally now finds her dentures quite comfortable.

Barbara H., Bruxism, and Chronic Pain

This 48 year-old woman came to my office complaining that she unconsciously ground her teeth at night and now had to have several teeth capped. She said she was afraid she would continue grinding her teeth and wear out the new caps.

Since bruxism or grinding of the teeth usually has a psychogenic etiology, hypnotherapy was indicated. I contacted Barbara's dentist who agreed that hypnotherapy might help his patient and asked that I treat her.

Barbara was optimistic about the results of hypnotherapy but harbored many misconceptions about hypnosis. After thoroughly explaining what hypnosis was not and performing a variety of suggestibility tests, I arranged for Barbara to come back to my office on the following day for therapy.

Prior to beginning our first session, Barbara told me that in addition to grinding her teeth she also suffered from chronic neck pain and was seeing a chiropractor who was treating her for an old neck injury. As the therapeutic goal for the first visit was to relieve her bruxism, I deferred working with her chronic pain problem until I could consult with her chiropractor.

I induced a light state of hypnosis and then guided Barbara to a medium state of hypnosis using the yardstick deepening technique. I elected to employ a nondirective approach for Barbara's bruxism. This technique is well documented in Dr. Irene Hickman's outstanding book, "Mind Probe Hypnosis."

This nondirective technique assumes that the patient knows the unconscious cause of their problem and can recall events or circumstances surrounding the problem. When the cause of the patient's problem and other factors are revivified with non directive therapy, the problem generally resolves itself.

I suggested to Barbara that she go back in time, as far back as necessary until she found the reason for grinding her teeth. She was extremely quiet for several moments and then appeared to be agitated and began moaning. I then suggested to Barbara that the cause of her problem would become clearer as I counted from five back to one and on the numeral one she would be able to tell me what she was experiencing. The following is a synopsis of her remarks during this session.

"I am frightened, I want to help but I don't know what to do." Barbara continued to explain the events that occurred fifteen years earlier on a summer evening.

Apparently her husband was having an emotional breakdown and was pleading for help in their living room while the children watched and asked their mother what they should do. This devoted wife and mother felt lost and useless because she didn't know what to do.

She gave her husband some medication his psychiatrist had prescribed, but that only seemed to make matters worse. The husband threatened to harm himself or her and then called the police for help. Eventually an ambulance took her husband to a psychiatric unit at a local hospital.

"He kept calling me from the hospital, begging me to get him out of there. I was so frustrated, angry and felt like a failure." Barbara cried with great emotion as she talked about that night years ago.

I asked Barbara if she still felt frightened and fearful about that night. She said yes, so I gently guided her back to that night and asked her to tell me about it again. This time she was less tearful and much more calm. She recalled the events in even greater detail. Since she was still feeling a small degree of fear, I asked her to tell me the story again.

The third time Barbara told the story she was calm and collected. Fear and frustration had left her voice and she even found some of the incidents humorous. When I asked her if she still felt any fear or frustration about that night, she replied "No."

I then suggested that she let go of that night and no longer needed or had a desire to feel fearful or frustrated since that evening was many years ago.

Upon awakening, Barbara did not recall any of her remarks during the therapy session. She listened intently as I played back a recording of the session To the best of my knowledge, Barbara has not had another episode of bruxism.

Was this evening fifteen years earlier really the cause of Barbara's bruxism? I honestly don't know. I do know that Barbara found a way within her own mind to solve the problem and that is more important than trying to prove how hypnotherapy helped or why it worked.

I consulted Barbara's chiropractor regarding her chronic neck pain before scheduling a second appointment with her. The chiropractor concurred with my belief that guided imagery might be beneficial. He gave me a brief report over the phone as to his patient's current condition and the therapeutic modalities he was using to help her with her neck pain. He agreed to mail me a letter requesting hypnotherapy for Barbara.

During our second session, Barbara revealed that her job was very stressful and that she spent hours talking on the phone. Her neck pain seemed to be worse at work and on nights when she found it difficult to sleep.

I suggested Pain or Anxiety as the Object imagery during our session for immediate alleviation of her neck pain and safe place imagery to help her relax at the end of the day. I instructed her in the application of self-hypnosis for stress and tension. I provided Barbara with appropriate therapeutic reinforcement tapes which she listened to daily for the next month.

Postscript

Barbara has been able to significantly alleviate her chronic neck pain with self-hypnosis techniques for the past year. Her chiropractor reports that her condition has responded well to his therapy and feels that guided imagery has had a significant role in improving the quality of his patient's life.

Dear Dr. Longacre,

"Hypnotic natural childbirth was a marvelous experience. I still use self-hypnosis when I feel stressed and need to relax."

Kathy S.

"I use self-hypnosis and just go fishing while I'm in the dental chair."

Paul D.

"My dentures are so comfortable and I don't have a problem with gagging anymore."

Sally M.

"I don't grind my teeth and best of all, I can manage my neck pain and have learned how to really relax."

Barbara H.

Index of Imagery Scripts

About the Author

■

R.D. Longacre, Ph.D., F.B.H.A., has over thirty years of experience as an allied health professional, educator, clinician and hypnotherapy specialist in the area of visualization and guided imagery for pain management.

Upon completion of his medical studies at the University of California, Irvine, Medical Center as a Neonatal Respiratory Care Practitioner, he elected to pursue further training in the area of psychotherapy and hypnotherapy. He has completed internships in psychotherapy and hypnotherapy and has earned doctoral degrees in both Cognitive Sciences and Hypnotherapy.

Dr. Longacre is a Diplomate of the American Institute of Hypnotherapy and a Fellow of the National Board for Hypnotherapy and Hypnotic Anaesthesiology. He is a Past Chairman of the Council of Professional Hypnosis Organizations, Past President of the American Board of Hypnotherapy and a Past Member of the Board of Directors for several prestigious hypnotherapy associations including the National Society of Hypnotherapists.

Dr. Longacre is the Administrator of the National Board for Hypnotherapy and Hypnotic Anaesthesiology, a division of NBHA, Inc., and the President of the American Association of Catastrophic Illness Counselors.

Dr. Longacre's efforts on behalf of hypnotherapists has made it possible for members of the National Board for Hypnotherapy and Hypnotic Anaesthesiology to receive third party reimbursement for hypnotherapy services billed to insurance companies.

Dr. Longacre has received awards from almost every nationally recognized hypnotherapy organization and was inducted into the

International Hypnosis Hall of Fame in 1991 for his outstanding contributions to hypnotherapy research and education.

Dr. Longacre resides in Arizona, where his private practice is limited to hypnotic anaesthesia and pain management in medical or surgical settings.

Other Books By
Dr. R.D. Longacre

∎

Available From Kendall/Hunt Publishing Company

CLIENT-CENTERED HYPNOTHERAPY

This new edition contains 47 classical imagery scripts and Client-Centered Inductions developed by Dr. R.D. Longacre for professional therapists who incorporate hypnosis into their counseling and teaching sessions.

A special chapter on behavior modification for weight control helps the therapist dispel the myths of the "Great Weight Lie" and develop a more effetive treatment plan for patients who wish to change eating habits and enjoy life with a positive attitude about themselves and others.

This best selling book is recommended reading for health care professionals and hypnotherapists who work with pain management clients or patients.

To order, call or write:
Kendall/Hunt Publishing Company
4050 Westmark Drive
P.O. Box 1840
Dubuque, Iowa 52004-1840
Phone: 1-800-228-0810
FAX: 1-800-772-9165

To insure good health; eat lightly, breathe deeply, live moderately, cultivate cheerfulness, and maintain an interest in Life.
——William Louden

Hypno depthmeter — 70, 83

Dissociation   85